FOOD FESTIVALS
of Texas

TRAVELER'S GUIDE
AND
COOKBOOK

Bob Carter

FALCON®

Helena, Montana

Design, typesetting, and other prepress work by Falcon Publishing®, Helena, Montana.

Printed in Canada.

Library of Congress Cataloging-in-Publication Data

Carter, Bob, 1932–
     Food festivals of Texas : traveler's guide and
cookbook / Bob Carter.
          p.   cm.
     Includes index
     ISBN 1-56044-843-1 (pbk.)
     1. Cookery, American—Southwestern style.   2. Festivals—Texas
     —Guidebooks.   I. Title.
TX715.2   .S69 C375   1999
641.59764—dc21   98-50183
                                                            CIP

CONTENTS

CONTENTS

ACKNOWLEDGMENTS

Creating a book like this requires the participation and support of many people. I am indebted to dozens of wonderful, friendly Texans who willingly shared festival information and delightful recipes with me. These generous contributors are recognized in appropriate places throughout this book. I hope their Texas-size hospitality and invaluable input is reflected in these pages. A few people deserve special mention and thanks.

Kimberly Baker, U.S./Canada Project Coordinator, Texas Department of Economic Development, Tourism Division, helped lead the way by providing details for the "Texas Regional Highlights" section and an extensive list of Texas festivals and celebrations. Once again Terry Poland came through as a computer champ and an indispensable resource assistant. My thanks, too, go to Megan Hiller, Senior Editor extraordinaire, for her encouragement and support.

INTRODUCTION

Texas Doing and Dining

The mere mention of its name conjures up visions of cowboys, rodeos, barbecues, and hot chili. All these, and more, are celebrated with gusto by Texas residents and visitors. The state is home to hundreds of festivals celebrating Texas, its heritage, and some of the best "gosh durn" food on the planet! Texans love to have a good time. Give them an excuse and they'll organize a noteworthy event and invite the world to attend. Hopefully, this book reflects some of the most flavorful events and food the state has to offer.

Every year tens of thousands of Texas residents and visitors take time to attend one or more of the state's eclectic array of food-oriented festivals and culinary celebrations. From the smallest of rural communities to the sophistication and diversity of large urban areas, hundreds of hometown celebrations offering fun for all take place every season of the year.

These varied events provide family-style entertainment, gourmet restaurant samplings, and some of the best homemade tastes found anywhere. It's not a bad idea to plan to attend them all! What I've tried to do in this book is provide you with information and recipes from a sampling of representative festivals and events. My hope is that they'll inspire you to hit the road, find others, and fill your life with exciting travel experiences and culinary delights.

If I've missed your favorite, or you want to contact me, I'd love to hear from you. Write me in care of Falcon Publishing, Inc., P.O. Box 1718, Helena, Montana 59624.

If you're so inclined, plan your traveling schedule to include one or more of my favorite events. If you do, you'll sample some of the most extraordinary food and meet some of the most friendly and neighborly people that Texas has to offer.

Happy trails and bon appétit!

USING THIS BOOK

For many travelers, attending a local festival or celebration helps make a trip more memorable. Texas has a plethora of wonderful events that celebrate the state's diversity and heritage. *Food Festivals of Texas: Traveler's Guide And Cookbook* provides festival information that strikes a balance between rural and urban, large and small, and free and more costly.

Although some of the recipes have been adapted slightly for consistency in format, I've tried to allow each contributor's personality to shine through. Whenever you see a chef's hat, you'll obtain some insight into the recipe. When I've felt the need to add my bit of personal observation, you'll find it designated with a small writing pad and pen.

ORGANIZATION OF FESTIVALS: The events detailed in this book are arranged alphabetically by festival name, followed by city or county location. No more than one festival for each location has been described in detail.

FURTHER FEASTINGS: Because most communities and regions hold several food-oriented events during the year, only one such event has been selected to include in the main portion of this book. When available, additional events have been listed in the *Further Feastings* section with the name of the event, city, and contact number provided.

INFORMATION DIRECTORY: It is strongly suggested you write, call, fax, or e-mail for additional information regarding destinations and events. The *Information Directory* portion of this guide includes contacts for individual festivals, event sponsors, chambers of commerce, and/or visitor bureaus. These agencies will furnish details regarding accommodations, dining, shopping, recreation, attractions, and additional special events and festivals.

TEXAS CELEBRATIONS: A *Texas Events Calendar* is published quarterly by the Travel and Information Division of the Texas Department of Transportation.

Information in the calendar is supplied by Texas chambers of commerce. Information about additional events is available locally through each city's chamber of commerce and visitor bureau. To receive your free copy of *Texas Events Calendar*, write to the Texas Department of Transportation, P.O. Box 5064, Austin, Texas 78763.

SPECIAL NOTE: Although diligent effort has been made to confirm the accuracy of information contained in this work, neither the publisher nor the author is responsible for errors, inaccuracies, or changes occurring after publication. Event offerings sometimes change. To avoid disappointment, it's strongly suggested that you confirm festival dates, fees, locations, and specific activities in advance.

TEXAS REGIONAL HIGHLIGHTS

One thing's for sure: Texas is big. It's like a whole other country. Almost 800 miles wide, the state contains nearly twenty million of the friendliest people you're ever likely to meet. It seems they enjoy nothing more than getting together and celebrating Texas's bounty and regional diversity.

With a land and water area of approximately 266,807 square miles, Texas occupies about seven percent of the total land and water area of the United States. This fact makes Texas the second-largest state in the country, behind Alaska. Texas is bordered on the east by Arkansas, Louisiana, and the Gulf of Mexico, on the north by Oklahoma, on the west by New Mexico, and on the south by Mexico.

Texas's size provides a variety of geographical regions, each with its own distinct characteristics. To assist visitors in their travels, the Texas Department of Economic Development, Tourism Division has divided the state into the following seven territories.

PINEY WOODS

The Piney Woods extends into Texas from the east 75 to 125 miles and to the south from the Red River to within 25 miles of the Gulf Coast. With its abundance of rainfall (40 to 55 inches a year), this area is characterized by moist woodlands and swamps, and with its millions of acres of pine forests, it's the source of practically all of Texas's large commercial timber production.

In addition to being the source of the state's timber industry, the state's four national forests—which offer wonderful camping, hiking, fishing, and hunting—are located in this densely wooded region. These forests, which comprise more than 600,000 acres, are known as Angelina, Davy Crockett, Sabine, and Sam Houston.

Quaint historic towns and replica pioneer settlements such as Rusk, Mount Pleasant, Palestine, Jefferson, and Tyler lie within the Piney Woods area. These small-town communities are popular travel destinations filled with antique shops, galleries, historic homes and buildings, and delightful bed-and-breakfast inns.

Also in this region is Nacogdoches, which showcases some of Texas's most historic landmarks. Huntsville, one of the state's oldest cities, is home to the 66-foot-high Sam Houston statue—the world's tallest statue of an American hero.

The Piney Woods area boasts nineteen state parks including Tyler, Rusk/Palestine, Texas State Railroad, and Parks State Park. In addition, numerous lakes, reservoirs, and bird-watching sites dot the landscape. Scenic drives throughout this area offer excellent woodland scenery and colorful Texas wildflowers.

PRAIRIES AND LAKES

The Prairies and Lakes region includes several distinct geographic areas occupying the north-central section of the state between the Panhandle Plains region to the west and the Piney Woods region to the east. These areas include the Post Oak Belt, Blackland Belt, Grand Prairie, and East and West Cross Timbers. These distinct locations feature rolling prairies, numerous streams, and soils easily adapted for fruit, vegetable, cotton, and livestock production. This region of the state is the most densely populated.

The Metroplex area includes Dallas, Fort Worth, and surrounding communities. Dallas offers its visitors exciting night life, outstanding cultural arts, museums, a symphony, the ballet, and more shopping centers per capita than any city in the United States. Fort Worth, known as Cow Town to many, provides a more authentic flavor of the Wild West.

Located between Dallas and Fort Worth are several smaller cities, including Irving, Grand Prairie, and Arlington. These communities provide sports buffs and families with all types of professional sporting teams, amusement parks, and shopping opportunities.

South of the Metroplex is a variety of cities rich in history and home to internationally recognized universities. Baylor University, the Dr. Pepper Museum, and the Texas Rangers Hall of Fame and Museum are located in Waco. Further south, College Station features the George Bush Presidential Library, located on the campus of Texas A&M University.

The Prairies and Lakes region is home to thirty-three state parks, including Pedernales Falls, Dinosaur Valley, Bastrop, Cedar Hill, Eisenhower, and Mother Neff, the first state park in Texas.

GULF COAST

The Texas Gulf Coast region extends along the Gulf of Mexico from the Sabine River to the Lower Rio Grande Valley and reaches inland 30 to 60 miles. The eastern half of the region is covered with a heavy growth of grass; the western half is covered with short grass and, in some places, with small timber and brush.

Major cities, hideaway resorts, and beautiful wildlife refuges dot the more-than-600-mile stretch of beaches. Houston, the largest city in the state, and one of the nation's largest seaports, hosts performing arts, concerts, sports events, and family amusement parks. The Lyndon B. Johnson Space Center is located in Houston as well.

The resort islands and coastal cities of South Padre Island, Corpus Christi, Galveston, and Port Aransas offer relaxing beach vacations, boating, windsurfing, and deep-sea fishing. Other attractions include Galveston's historic Strand District, Moody Gardens, and the Port Isabel Lighthouse. The "Ships of Christopher Columbus" replicas and the U.S.S. *Lexington* are harbored in Corpus Christi. Brownsville and its sister city, Matamoros, Mexico, display the ambiance of Old Mexico with its popular marketplace, mariachis, and Mexican cuisine.

Home to twenty state parks, the Gulf Coast is also a popular bird-watching and camping destination. Enjoyable year-round, the 110-mile-long Padre Island is one of the longest natural seashores in the nation.

SOUTH TEXAS PLAINS

The South Texas Plains region features geographical characteristics of both the Texas Gulf Coast Plain and the North Mexico Plains. They have similar topography, climate, and plant life. Similar to Mexico in many ways, the region includes historic missions, mariachis, and working ranches. Many of the cultural activities are influenced by Mexico.

Throughout San Antonio, Del Rio, Laredo, and other South Texas cities, historic battle sites of Texas's independence reside side-by-side with the modern urban sights of metropolitan shops, tastes of international cuisine, and popular nightclubs. The natural border of the Rio Grande River is all that separates the south Texas cities of Laredo and McAllen from their sister cities of Nuevo Laredo, and Meynosa, Mexico. This proximity adds to the rich culture of this historic, Mexican-influenced region.

Because of the rich delta soils and the normal absence of freezing weather, the Lower Rio Grand Valley is Texas's greatest area for growing citrus and winter vegetables. The mild winter temperatures also make this region a haven for many northern travelers. Known as "snowbirds" and "Winter Texans," this group of globetrotters travels to the area to escape the harsh winters of the northern U.S.

HILL COUNTRY

The Hill Country is the popular name for an area of hills and spring-fed streams along the northern edge of the Balcones Escarpment. Notable large springs include Barton Springs in Austin, San Marcos Springs in San Marcos, Comal Springs in New

Braunfels, and several springs in San Antonio. Edwards Plateau is also a part of this region.

In addition to being home to scenic natural beauty, the Hill Country is also a perfect place to enjoy historical and contemporary sightseeing. Among the many attractions are the capital city of Austin, Lyndon B. Johnson National Historical Park in Johnson City, and the Admiral Nimitz Museum and Historical Center in Fredericksburg.

Austin's reputation as the live-music capital of the world is well deserved. Live entertainment is featured there seven days a week. Festivals are one main attraction in this region and include Wurstfest in New Braunfels, Oktoberfest, celebrated by many of the German-influenced communities, and Aquafest, held in Austin each summer.

Springtime in this region attracts thousands of people who come to see the bluebonnets and other wildflowers growing along state highways and in open fields. The Hill Country is a popular summer destination offering river tubing down the Guadalupe and San Marcos rivers.

Small communities, such as New Braunfels, Gruene, Fredericksburg, and San Marcos, are steeped in European tradition and are popular for antique shopping, international cuisine, and fine Texas wines. Area accommodations include historic bed-and-breakfast inns along with quaint and contemporary hotels.

Nature lovers enjoy the Hill Country's twenty-one beautiful state parks including Enchanted Rock State Natural Area, McKinney Falls, Inks Lake, and Guadalupe River. Scenic drives throughout the Hill Country along Lake Travis, Lake Marble Falls, and the Pecos River are some of the most picturesque in Texas.

PANHANDLE PLAINS

The Texas Panhandle stretches over the largest level plain of its kind in the United States. The area rises gradually from about 2,700 feet on the east to more than 4,000 feet in spots along the New Mexico border. Major cities here include Amarillo, Abilene, Lubbock, and San Angelo. Known for its rugged, Texas-cowboy personality, the region is famous for hunting, fishing, and shopping, and its ranches, frontier settlements, and rich Texas culture.

The Panhandle is home to fourteen state parks including Palo Duro Canyon, one of the state's largest parks. One of the most impressive drives in the region is along Texas Highway 207. For miles, agricultural riches spread from horizon to horizon and then plunge into the scenic grandeur of Palo Duro Canyon's steep cliffs and colorful canyons.

BIG BEND COUNTRY

Big Bend Country contains the Davis Mountains and the Big Bend area, so called because it is bordered on three sides by the great southward swing of the Rio Grande. The principal mountains of the area, the Chisos, rise to 7,825 feet. The southern part of the area is along the Rio Grande and home to Big Bend National Park. The variation in temperatures results in vast plant and animal life. More than 450 bird species have been observed in the area, along with ringtails, black bears, and mountain lions.

River Road, one of the most spectacular drives in Texas, plunges over mountains and canyons along the sun-drenched Rio Grande. The region contains fourteen state parks providing hunting, fishing, bird watching, camping, and hiking.

The largest city in Big Bend Country is El Paso, a 400-year-old town rich in Mexican heritage. The Midland/Odessa area originally was settled during the oil boom in 1919. Today these sister cities have grown and developed with high-rise buildings, a strong educational system, and dedication to the fine arts. Terlingua, near Big Bend, is home of the world-renowned International Championship Chili Cookoff, held every November and attended by thousands of "hot heads."

Visitor Information: Even the free official *Texas State Travel Guide* is enormous. Its nearly 300 pages provide a colorful look into the state's large urban areas and rural communities. To receive your personal copy of this coffee-table-quality guide, call 800-8888-TEX. If you love celebrations, request the free *Texas Events Calendar* also.

LOCATOR MAP

THE FESTIVALS

1 Alley Oop Chili & BBQ Cookoff, Iraan
2 Apple Butter Festival, Idalou
3 Bar-B-Q Festival, Vidor
4 Black-Eyed Pea Jamboree, Athens
5 Blueberry Festival, Nacogdoches County
6 Border Folk Festival, El Paso
7 Butterfield Stage Days, Bridgeport
8 Charro Days, Brownsville
9 Chilympiad, San Marcos
10 Citrus Fiesta, Mission
11 Corn Festival, Holland
12 Cotton Pickin' Fair & Go Texan Days, Hillsboro
13 Crawfish Festival, Mauriceville
14 Dairy Festival & Ice Cream Freeze-off, Sulphur Springs
15 Fall Festival & World Champion Stew Contest, Hopkins County
16 Fiery Foods Show, Austin
17 Folklife Festival, San Antonio
18 General Granbury's Birthday Party and Bean Cook-Off, Granbury
19 General Sam Houston Folk Festival, Huntsville
20 Germanfest, Muenster
21 Hill Country Wine & Food Festival, Austin
22 International Apple Festival, Medina
23 International Gumbo Cook-off, Orange
24 Jalapeño Festival, Laredo
25 Mex-Tex Menudo Cook Off, Midland
26 Oktoberfest, Fredericksburg
27 Onion Festival, Weslaco

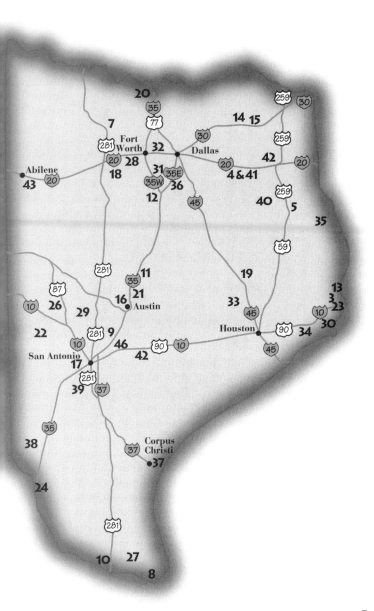

ALLEY OOP CHILI & BBQ COOKOFF

IRAAN

Annual. First Saturday in June.

Attention all Alley Oop aficionados. Here's your chance to don your jeans, cowboy boots, and Stetson hats, and join in celebrating the life and times of your favorite comic hero. The day's filled with Alley, Miss Oola, Little Miss Pebbles, and BamBam. Besides, you'll have a chance to taste some of the best chili and barbecue around.

The event was named for the comic strip caveman, Alley Oop, because V. T. Hamlin, creator of the Alley Oop comics, once lived in Iraan and is still revered by residents and visitors. So are his human- and dinosaur-like creations. In the 1920s, while working on other projects, Hamlin came upon the idea of Alley Oop. His creative characters come alive during the city's unique annual festival.

The main events occur on Saturday but begin with the selection on Friday night of Miss Oola, Little Miss Pebbles, and Mr. Alley Oop Caveman. The winners are honored and ride in the carefree parade held on Saturday morning. The parade is filled with bands, horse units, fun-loving participants, and the Alley Oop float carrying the hand-waving dignitaries.

Held in the forty-acre city park, the revelers meet to enjoy arts-and-crafts vendors, food booths, games, and just about anything else anyone can dream up to create excitement and competitions. Fantasyland Park, adjacent to the festival site, is open free for everyone to enjoy. Giant statues immortalize Oop, his girl friend Oola, and his dinosaur, Dinny. Dinny is sixty-five feet long, sixteen feet tall, and 80,000 pounds heavy. Bring your camera because a favorite spot for snapshots is astride Dinny's head or sliding out of Oop's twenty-foot top hat.

Come prepared to enjoy the cook-off, too. The competition categories include chili, beans, brisket, pork spareribs, and chicken. All entries are judged by professional barbecue and chili association criteria. You'll want to eat hearty and savor the quality food available throughout the day.

In the afternoon, professional riders compete during the Alley Oop Bull Ride competitions in a small rodeo atmosphere. Following the excitement of the bull-riding activities, everyone relaxes to some fine entertainment at the Alley Oop dance held in the park under the stars.

Iraan, Alley Oop, and all his friends are located 13 miles north of Interstate Highway 10 on Texas Highway 349.

TEXAS CHILI

Brown meat with onion and garlic approximately 30 minutes. Add tomato sauce, water, and 1 tablespoon chili powder. Add jalapeños; let them float in the chili. Boil slowly for about an hour. Add rest of chili powder (to taste), bouillon cubes, cayenne pepper, and black pepper. Stir, simmer for 45 minutes. Add 2 tablespoons cumin, salt to taste, 1 tablespoon Crisco (for grainy texture), and water if necessary. Slow simmer until ready to serve.

Alley Oop Chili & BBQ Cookoff
Iraan, Texas

3 pounds chili-grind
hamburger

1 onion, diced

1 fresh garlic clove, ground to
pulp

1 8-ounce can tomato sauce

2 8-ounce cans water

6 to 8 tablespoons chili
powder, to taste

2 jalapeños

2 beef bouillon cubes

2 chicken bouillon cubes

$\frac{1}{2}$ teaspoon cayenne pepper

$\frac{1}{2}$ teaspoon black pepper

2 tablespoons cumin

salt to taste

1 tablespoon Crisco

water

FESTIVAL OF THE WEST'S COWBOY CHILI

2 pounds dried pinto beans (or 4 16-ounce cans pinto beans)

2 medium onions, chopped

4 tablespoons chili powder (optional)

$\frac{1}{2}$ cup brown sugar

2 pounds diced beef (London Broil makes excellent chili)

1 medium green pepper, diced

$\frac{1}{2}$ cup chopped celery

1 clove garlic, crushed

30 ounces canned Mexican-style stewed tomatoes

21$\frac{1}{2}$ ounces canned tomato soup

6 ounces canned whole kernel corn

4 ounces canned diced green chilies (optional)

Soak beans overnight, drain, and place in Dutch oven. Add water to cover by 1 inch, add onions, chili powder, and brown sugar. Cook over medium-low heat for 3 to 4 hours or until tender, being certain to add water as necessary. In skillet with small amount of oil, brown beef, green pepper, chopped celery, and garlic together; add to beans. Add remaining ingredients. Heat to serving temperature.

Festival of the West
Scottsdale, Arizona

 Excellent with cornbread or crackers with plenty of butter.

GETTY UP CHILI

Sauté onion in olive oil until soft, add meat and cook until reddish color is gone. Stir in tomatoes, mix in chili powder, garlic, celery seed, salt and pepper. Simmer for 1 hour. Add vinegar and brown sugar, and mix well. Add sausage and heat to serving temperature.

Patty Fessenden
Mission, Texas

1 large onion, chopped

3 tablespoons olive oil

$^3/_4$ pound lean beef, chopped

5 large ripe tomatoes, peeled, chopped

3 tablespoons chili powder or to taste

3 cloves garlic, crushed

$^1/_2$ teaspoon celery seed

salt and pepper to taste

2 tablespoons vinegar

2 tablespoons brown sugar

1 pound Italian sausage, peeled, chopped, cooked

JIFFY TAMALE CHILI

¹/₄ cup minced onion

¹/₄ cup chopped green pepper

1 tablespoon butter or margarine

2 cups canned chili con carne with beans

11 ounces canned tamales

¹/₂ cup shredded sharp cheese

Cook onion and green pepper in butter until tender but not brown. Add chili. Remove shucks from tamales, arrange spoke-fashion on top. Cover and heat 10 to 15 minutes. Sprinkle with shredded cheese before serving.

Tweet Brumaghim
El Cajon, California

You get real Mexican flavor fast with this combination of canned specialties, onion, green pepper, and sharp cheese. Serve with a garden salad and your yummy dinner is ready.

APPLE BUTTER FESTIVAL

IDALOU

Annual. September weekend (seasonal).

2

Pack up the family and head to Idalou, Texas. If one a day keeps the doctor away, then you'll experience enough apple-related, frolicking fun to last for years at the annual Apple Butter Festival. Go ahead, invite your doctor. Here's your chance to enjoy a benefit barbecue lunch with all the trimmings, taste some of the best apple turnovers and ice cream in the country, and be delighted by lively entertainment including barbershop singing groups, pianists, and ethnic dancers. It's all available in the shade of apple trees on a sunny West Texas fall weekend.

The site of the festival, Apple Country at Hi Plains Orchards, is the perfect casual environment for a celebration of the apple season. Not only will you be able to pick your own juicy apples, but you'll have a chance to savor live music, sip cold cider, stroll past craft booths, join the square dancing, and more. The weekend's events include live bluegrass, country, and gospel music, square dancing, cowboy poetry, huge vats of boiling apple butter, and more.

The barbecue brisket lunch with all the fixin's is one of the major food highlights. However, you'll want to save room to participate in the hilarious apple-pie-eating contests and load up on apple-based bakery goods, jams, jellies, and honey fresh from on-site hives.

While the apple takes center stage during the Apple Butter Festival, you can also pick black-eyed peas, okra, tomatoes, and peppers. Truly "picker friendly," the orchard comes alive with families sharing the fruits and vegetables of the season. It's a special treat to take the horse-drawn wagon rides that wind through the orchard and its 6,000 apple trees.

It's the West Texas sunshine that causes local apples to have up to 40 percent more sugar than apples grown elsewhere. You'll go away convinced that tree-ripened apples are better by far than supermarket apples which have been picked months before their flavors have peaked.

The Apple Butter Festival is a family-oriented, fun-packed weekend celebrating the season and raising money to benefit the local Rotary Club's South Plains Food Bank. You'll have so much fun and mouth-watering items to taste, you'll keep the memories of your visit for a lifetime.

Apple Country at Hi Plains Orchards is located 4 miles east of Idalou and 15 miles east of Lubbock on U.S. Highway 62/82.

All recipes for this section provided by the Apple Butter Festival.

CHUNKY APPLE PANCAKES

In a bowl, stir together flour, baking powder, salt, and sugar. In a separate bowl, beat egg, milk, and oil together; pour all at once into dry ingredients. Stir until smooth, then mix in chopped apples. If using electric griddle, preheat to 375°. If using stove griddle, use medium heat. Spoon about $1/4$ cup of mix onto griddle. Cook until pancake is brown, then turn and cook until the other side is brown. Serve with Apple Spiced Topping. Recipe follows.

Topping: Steam apples, sugar, and cinnamon until apples are tender. Stir often to avoid scorching. Spoon onto hot pancakes.

 A favorite to serve during the festival or anytime of year. This pancake mix is filled with lots of fresh chunks of apple.

1 cup unsifted, all-purpose flour

2 teaspoons baking powder

1 teaspoon salt

$1/4$ cup sugar

1 egg

$1/3$ cup milk

2 teaspoons oil

2 medium-sized apples, peeled, finely chopped

Apple Spiced Topping

4 medium-sized apples, sliced (peel if desired)

$1/4$ cup sugar

1 teaspoon cinnamon

APPLE-MAPLE STUFFING

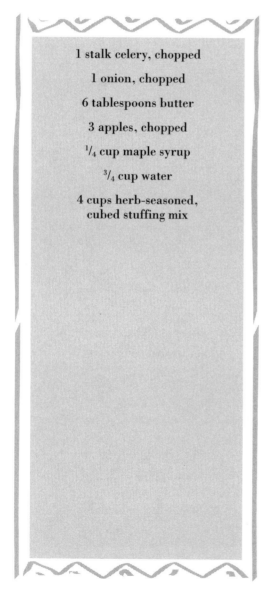

1 stalk celery, chopped

1 onion, chopped

6 tablespoons butter

3 apples, chopped

$^1/_4$ cup maple syrup

$^3/_4$ cup water

4 cups herb-seasoned, cubed stuffing mix

Simmer celery and onion in 4 tablespoons butter for 2 minutes. Add apples and remaining butter, simmer additional 2 minutes. Add syrup and water, bring to a boil. Pour stuffing mix into a large bowl, add hot mixture and stir well. Sufficient stuffing for a 6 to 10 pound goose or any bird.

WALDORF SALAD

Mix all salad ingredients together. Mix all dressing ingredients together. Pour dressing over salad and mix thoroughly. Cover and chill for at least 1 hour before serving.

Salad

6 apples, chopped

3 tablespoons lemon juice

$5^{1}/_{2}$ ounces canned pineapple, drained, chopped

$^{3}/_{4}$ cup chopped pecans

6 stalks celery, chopped

Dressing

$^{1}/_{2}$ cup mayonnaise

$^{1}/_{3}$ cup sour cream

1 teaspoon sugar or honey

WILD RICE AND APPLE SALAD

2 cups cooked wild rice
(approximately $1/2$ cup uncooked)

2 cups unpeeled, chopped apples,
green and red

2 stalks celery, chopped

Dressing

1 tablespoon brown sugar

$1/2$ cup plain yogurt

$1/4$ cup mayonnaise

Mix cooked rice, apples, and celery together. In a small bowl mix brown sugar, yogurt, and mayonnaise together well. Pour over rice mixture. Serve chilled.

BAR-B-Q FESTIVAL
VIDOR
Annual. Third weekend in May.

3

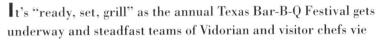

It's "ready, set, grill" as the annual Texas Bar-B-Q Festival gets underway and steadfast teams of Vidorian and visitor chefs vie for top prizes and awards during the cook-off. Organized by the Vidor Chamber of Commerce, the event is held at Conn Park. It's a weekend where friendly neighbors welcome visitors and the culinary climate is hot.

The main calling card of the event, the Texas Bar-B-Q Festival Championship Cook-Off, takes place Saturday evening and all day Sunday. Cookers prepare their culinary offerings throughout the night. They slave over hot, steaming pits in hopes of capturing the first-place trophy and prize money. Their gastro-secrets are often in the sauce.

The judging takes place Sunday afternoon. The competitive good nature and humor of the team members is reflected in the names of current and past participants. You can choose which teams you'll support during their cooking endeavors. Will it be "The No Cry Babies Gang," "Inlaws & Outlaws," "Texas Vittles," "Bushwacker Barbecue," or the "Mean, Lean Barbecue Team"? Heck, you're welcome to take the easy way out and support them all.

Early Saturday morning folks begin lining the Bar-B-Q Festival Parade route. There's a whole bunch of kith and kin there to cheer on the year's Queen and King, the Vidor High School and Junior High School marching bands, dozens of dignitaries, performers, and local clubs and service organizations.

Participating area businesses compete in, and are judged on, decorating their establishments. Their employees get into the act—and often the parade—dressed in

Texas attire. After the parade, it's special to stroll past colorful store fronts and admire their distinctive adornment.

Another unique aspect of the Vidor festival is the Treasure Hunt. The hunt begins with clues to the treasure's whereabouts posted at the chamber of commerce office on the Monday before the festival begins. Each day a new clue is posted until the treasure is found, and the crowning touch is the awarding of the much-sought-after prize.

Vidor is located on the Neches River between Beaumont and Orange on Interstate 10.

BARBECUING BEEF

How can you tell if beef is cooked to the doneness you prefer? According to the Texas Beef Council, there are several ways, depending upon the cut. For steaks and other thin cuts that are broiled, pan-broiled, or grilled, the easiest way to determine doneness is by cutting a small slit and checking the color of the meat near the bone or near the center of a boneless cut.

For roasts and thicker steaks (2 inches or more), using a thermometer is the preferred method of determining doneness. Two types of thermometers can be used: a meat thermometer, which is inserted into the roast prior to cooking and left in the roast during the entire cooking process; or an instant-read thermometer inserted for about ten seconds, then removed. An instant-read thermometer is not oven-safe. Use it toward the end of the minimum cooking time.

To determine doneness of steaks and roasts: Rare—center is bright red, pinkish toward outer portion; Medium—center is light pink, outer portion is brown; Well done—uniform gray/brown throughout. Recommended internal temperature for beef: rare 135°; medium-rare 140 to 145°; medium 150°; well-done 165°; ground beef 160 to 170°.

Texas Bar-B-Q Festival
Vidor, Texas

MARGARITA PORK KABOBS

1 cup margarita drink mix (or 1 cup lime juice, 4 teaspoons sugar, and $\frac{1}{2}$ teaspoon salt)

1 teaspoon ground coriander

1 clove garlic, minced

1 pound pork tenderloin, cut into 1-inch cubes

2 tablespoons butter, softened

2 tablespoons lime juice

$\frac{1}{8}$ teaspoon sugar

1 tablespoon minced fresh parsley

1 large green or red pepper, cut into 1-inch cubes

2 ears corn, each cut into 4 pieces

Combine margarita mix, coriander, and garlic. Place pork cubes in heavy plastic bag, pour marinade over to cover meat, and marinade for at least 30 minutes. Blend together the butter, lime juice, sugar, and parsley; set aside. Thread pork cubes onto skewers, alternating with pieces of corn and pepper. Grill over hot coals, basting with butter mixture, for 15 to 20 minutes. Baste and turn frequently.

National Pork Producers Council
Des Moines, Iowa

BARBECUED BEEF WITH CORN MUFFINS

Cut beef steaks crosswise into 1-inch wide strips. Sauté onions in oil in large skillet over medium-high heat until lightly browned. Remove onions and keep warm. Add beef strips to skillet, half at a time, and cook 2 to 3 minutes. Add barbecue sauce and onions, heat until hot. Serve over corn muffins.

Texas Beef Council
Austin, Texas

1 pound beef round tip steaks, cut $^{1}/_{8}$- to $^{1}/_{4}$- inch thick

1 medium onion, cut into thin wedges

2 teaspoons vegetable oil

$^{3}/_{4}$ cup barbecue sauce

4 corn muffins, quartered

CHERI'S SPICY BARBECUE SAUCE

1 tablespoon minced or
pressed garlic

1 large onion, finely chopped

1½ tablespoons olive oil

14 ounces canned crushed
tomatoes

⅓ cup tomato paste

¼ cup red wine vinegar

¼ cup Worcestershire sauce

1 bay leaf

1 tablespoon dried oregano

¼ teaspoon crushed red
pepper, or to taste

½ teaspoon dried thyme

1 teaspoon lemon juice

1 teaspoon lemon zest

¼ cup honey

Sauté garlic and onion in olive oil for about 3 to 5 minutes, or until tender. Stir in remaining ingredients and bring to a boil. Lower heat and simmer for about 30 minutes. Use for basting foods while grilling.

Cheri Sicard, Editor-in-Chief
Fabulous Foods On-line Magazine
www.fabulousfoods.com

 This is a spicy, thick, and chunky barbecue sauce. While it works great for the traditional grilled foods like chicken, ribs, or steak, I've also used it with great success on fish, especially salmon, and grilled vegetables of all kinds.

BLACK-EYED PEA JAMBOREE

ATHENS

Annual. Third weekend in July.

For many years, growing, processing, canning, and eating black-eyed peas was a major part of life in Athens. So much so, that Athens has become known as the "Black-eyed Pea Capital of the World." The residents take their peasponsibility seriously and constantly search out the most unique recipes and greatest cooks to help celebrate their yearly salute to the pea.

The black-eyed pea is a universal symbol of good luck. Also, according to legend, eating black-eyed peas on New Year's Day brings continuing good fortune throughout the coming year. So while you're there, pick up a pod of peas and prepare them for your next New Year's dinner.

Since 1971, a growing number of people have enjoyed the down-home flavor of three days of good, clean family fun. The popular Peas in the Park provides a wealth of activities for young and old. Arts-and-crafts booths are decked out in their finery, carnival sounds permeate the air, and dozens of runners participate in challenging 10K and 5K runs. There's even a terrapin race and an ever-popular pea-poppin' and pea-eatin' contest.

The giant draw for this event is the Black-Eyed Pea Cook-Off. You'll catch about 100 local and professional entrants preparing the likes of black-eyed pea torte, enchi-pea-ladas, pea-zza, pea-nutty salads, and other pea dishes that please the palate. You'll likely want to pick up the event's *Black-Eyed Pea Reci-Peas* cookbook and prepare some of your favorites at home.

Here's another tasty bit of Athens food information: The hamburger, a great American fast-food staple, was created by Fletcher Davis in the 1800s in a cafe on the Athens courthouse square.

Athens is located along Texas Highway 31, 75 miles southeast of Dallas; 189 miles north of Houston; and 36 miles west of Tyler.

PEA-LICIOUS CABBAGE CASSEROLE

1/2 stick margarine or butter

1 onion, chopped, divided

1 large head cabbage, chopped

1 1/2 pounds ground meat

10 ounces canned whole tomatoes

8 ounces canned tomato sauce

2 cups cooked rice

14 ounces canned black-eyed peas

10 3/4 ounces canned tomato soup

12 cheese slices

garlic salt, salt, and pepper to taste

Place 1/2 stick of butter in a Dutch oven. Add half of the chopped onion and all of the cabbage to Dutch oven; cover and steam until cabbage and onions are tender. In large skillet, brown meat and remaining chopped onion until brown. Add tomatoes and tomato sauce to meat mixture and simmer for 20 minutes.

In large, glass baking dish, alternate the following as indicated: 1 layer cabbage and onions, 1 layer meat sauce, 1 layer peas, and 1 layer rice. Arrange 6 cheese slices on top of rice. Add 1 layer cabbage and onions, 1 layer meat sauce, and canned tomato soup. Season to taste between layers. Arrange remaining black-eyed peas with 6 slices of cheese on top of casserole. Bake at 400° for 30 minutes, uncovered. Let stand 15 minutes, then serve.

Sheila Wedgeworth
Grand Champion Award
Tennessee Colony, Texas

HENDERSON COUNTY QUICHE

Use mashed peas to form a shell in a 10-inch pie plate which has been oiled with butter or margarine. Cook in 350° oven for 10 minutes. Place garlic, onion, ham, parsley, hot or sweet pepper, peas, and cheese in shell.

Combine eggs, milk, pea juice, black pepper, and sausage seasoning and mix thoroughly. Pour into shell over other ingredients. Cook in 350° oven about 30 minutes or until knife inserted in center comes out clean.

William Johnston
Grand Champion Award
Huntsville, Texas

2 to 3 cups cooked black-eyed peas (drained and mashed)

1 teaspoon garlic powder

$\frac{1}{2}$ cup finely chopped onion

1 cup chopped fine cooked ham (smoked hocks, etc.)

1 tablespoon chopped parsley

$\frac{1}{4}$ cup chopped hot or sweet pepper

$\frac{3}{4}$ cup cooked green black-eyed peas

1 cup shredded cheese

6 eggs, well beaten

1 cup evaporated milk

$\frac{1}{2}$ cup black-eyed pea juice

$\frac{1}{4}$ teaspoon black pepper

$1\frac{1}{2}$ teaspoons pork sausage seasoning

ROSEMARY CHICKEN AND BLACK-EYED PEAS EN CROUTE

8 ounces canned refrigerated crescent dinner rolls

2 tablespoons minced green onion

6 ounces mozzarella cheese, cubed

1½ cups chopped cooked chicken breast

1½ cups cooked and drained fresh black-eyed peas

1 egg, beaten

1 teaspoon crushed dried rosemary

1 tablespoon grated Parmesan cheese

1 medium tomato, cut into wedges, and 4 green onions for garnish if desired

Heat oven to 350°. Separate dough into 4 rectangles; firmly press perforations to seal. Spoon ¼ of minced green onion onto center of each rectangle, top with ¼ of cheese cubes, top each with ¼ of chicken, pressing into cheese. Add ¼ of the black-eyed peas to each. Fold over open ends about half an inch to form rectangle. Press all edges to seal. Place seam side down on ungreased cookie sheet. Cut three 1-inch slashes on top of each roll to allow steam to escape. Brush each roll with egg, sprinkle with rosemary and Parmesan cheese. Bake for 21 to 26 minutes or until golden brown. Let stand 5 minutes before serving.

Beau Stutts
Children's First Place Award
Athens, Texas

PEANIQUE ICE CREAM PIE

Crust: Melt butter. Mix butter and all but $1/2$ cup of the crumbled crackers together and press into 9-inch pie dish like a crust. Save $1/2$ cup of crackers for topping. Refrigerate to set mixture.

Filling: Let ice cream melt and mix packages of pudding into the melted ice cream. Mix until thick. Add whipped topping to mixture. Stir until all mixed together. Place black-eyed peas on crust, add ice cream mixture. Refrigerate for about 1 hour. Before serving sprinkle the remaining crackers on top.

Brenda Bettencourt
Grand Champion Award
Athens, Texas

This can be frozen if desired. If you prefer, you can use low-fat pudding for lower fat content.

Crust
1 stick butter or margarine

1 box Ritz crackers, crumbled

Filling
$1/2$ gallon vanilla ice cream

2 packages vanilla instant pudding

1 medium-size tub of whipped topping

1 cup cooked black-eyed peas

$1/2$ cup pecans, chopped

BLUEBERRY FESTIVAL

NACOGDOCHES COUNTY

Annual. June weekend.

5

The Texas Blueberry Festival is an exciting and entertaining celebration of the blueberry industry, and luscious desserts are a hallmark of the event. The festival kicks off on Friday with a Red, White, and Blue concert held in Eugenia Sterne Park located on Main Street. Bring the kids—they'll encounter plenty of children's games and activities. The musical entertainment begins at 7 P.M. and features a wide variety of brass bands, blues, and plenty of good ol' rock and roll.

Pack a picnic basket filled with plenty of food. It's traditional to bring your own meal to this special evening in the park. Concert goers are urged to bring lawn chairs or blankets to sit on. You'll find plenty of popcorn and soft drinks for sale at yesteryear prices.

After the concert, silent movies from the early days of Hollywood are shown under the stars. The clocks are turned back to the twenties, and the great stars of the silent movies are on hand to delight the audience with comedy, drama, tragedy, and suspense. You'll laugh at the antics of the Little Rascals, cheer for the guy in the white hat as he saves the damsel in distress, and boo the villain as he's foiled again. Charlie Chaplin will bring tears to your eyes as the Little Tramp struggles through life. You'll be amazed that the Keystone Cops don't wreck more cars. And, who knows, you may even see Laurel and Hardy in the crowd laughing along with you.

On Saturday, the festival gets underway with blueberry pancakes, arts and crafts booths, a petting zoo, and lots of fun for the entire family. The day's schedule is filled with an abundance of Texas delicacies. You can enjoy fresh blueberries, a pie-eating contest, and a fish fry. For live entertainment, catch the Miss Blueberry Pageant, watch a doll parade, or talk to the animals.

The streets of downtown Nacogdoches host the Blueberry Festival Doll Parade. If you have dolls or stuffed animals, whether live or not, bring them and join in the parade. It's designed to show them off dressed in their best bib and tucker.

Just before the Doll Parade, your pet gets a chance to shine. It's then that you can show off your beloved pet to all the festival participants. Remember, though, your pet must be leashed, in good health with current shots, and willing to get along with other pets.

If you love blueberries, here are a few of the many tempting treats you'll want to sample: fresh blueberries, blueberry pancakes, blueberry ice cream, and blueberry pie.

The Texas Blueberry Festival is a weekend of nonstop family activity.

Nacogdoches County is an eastern gateway into Texas. The city of Nacogdoches is located near where U.S. Highways 259 and 59 intersect.

All recipes in this section appear in *Blueberry Recipes from the Blueberry Place* by Nancy Metteauer, Nacogdoches resident.

BLUEBERRY STREUSEL COFFEE CAKE

Batter
2 cups all-purpose flour

$^3/_4$ cup sugar

2 teaspoons baking powder

$^1/_4$ teaspoon salt

1 egg, beaten

$^1/_2$ cup milk

$^1/_2$ cup butter or margarine, softened

1 banana, chopped, or 1 cup chopped pecans

1 cup blueberries

Streusel
$^1/_2$ cup sugar

$^1/_3$ cup all-purpose flour

$^1/_4$ cup cold butter or margarine

Batter: In a mixing bowl, combine flour, sugar, baking powder, and salt. Add egg, milk, and butter. Beat well. Fold in banana or pecans. Spread into a greased 8- or 9-inch square baking pan. Spread the blueberries evenly on top of batter. Using your hand or spatula, sink the blueberries slightly into the batter.

Streusel: In another bowl, combine sugar and flour; cut in the butter until crumbly. Sprinkle over the batter. Bake at 375° for 35 to 40 minutes or until a wooden pick inserted near the center comes out clean.

BLUEBERRY MUFFINS

Stir together flour, sugar, baking powder, baking soda, and salt. Make a well in the center of the dry ingredients. In another bowl, whisk the egg and then whisk in the buttermilk, vanilla, and melted butter or margarine. Pour egg mixture into dry ingredients. Quickly stir to partially blend. Add blueberries. Carefully fold together to moisten. The batter will be thick and lumpy. Spoon batter into 12 paper-lined muffin tins. The cups will be full. Sprinkle the tops with 1 tablespoon sugar. Bake 25 to 30 minutes at 400°. When done, the tops will spring back when lightly touched. Let cool in the pan for 5 minutes and then carefully remove and cool on a rack.

2 cups flour

$^1/_2$ cup sugar

1 tablespoon baking powder

$^1/_4$ teaspoon baking soda

$^1/_2$ teaspoon salt

1 large egg

1 cup buttermilk

1 teaspoon vanilla

5 tablespoons butter or margarine, melted

1$^1/_4$ cups blueberries

1 tablespoon sugar for topping

BLUEBERRY CREAM CHEESE POUND CAKE

Cake

8 ounces softened cream cheese

$^1/_2$ cup vegetable oil

1 yellow butter cake mix

1 small package instant vanilla
pudding mix

4 eggs, well beaten

2 teaspoons vanilla

2 cups blueberries

powdered sugar, optional

Blueberry Glaze

2 cups blueberries

$^1/_2$ cup water

$^1/_2$ cup sugar

2 tablespoons cornstarch

1 tablespoon lemon juice

Cake: Cream together cream cheese and oil. Stir in cake mix, pudding mix, eggs, and vanilla. Mix well. Fold in blueberries. Pour into prepared bundt pan. Bake 1 hour at 325°. Cool 20 minutes in pan.

Options: After baking, sprinkle with powdered sugar or fill center hole with blueberry glaze (recipe follows).

Glaze: Mix all ingredients in small saucepan. Bring to a slow boil and simmer for about 5 minutes. Great served over cheesecake, pound cake, pancakes, waffles, ice cream, or shortcake.

BLUEBERRY-LEMON BREAD

Cream butter and gradually add 1 cup sugar, beating at medium speed with an electric mixer until well-blended. Add eggs, one at a time, beating well after each addition. Combine flour, baking powder, and salt. Add to creamed mixture alternately with milk. Stir in grated lemon rind. Dredge blueberries in flour; fold into batter. Pour batter into a greased loaf pan. Bake at 350° for 55 minutes or until a wooden pick inserted in center comes out clean.

Combine $1/3$ cup sugar and lemon juice in a small saucepan. Heat until sugar dissolves. Puncture top of bread in several places with a wooden pick. Pour lemon juice mixture over warm bread, allowing mixture to soak into bread. Cool in the pan 30 minutes.

6 tablespoons butter or margarine

1 cup sugar

2 eggs

$1^1/_2$ cups flour

1 teaspoon baking powder

$1/_2$ teaspoon salt

$1/_2$ cup milk

2 teaspoons grated lemon rind

1 cup blueberries

2 teaspoons flour

$1/_3$ cup sugar

3 tablespoons lemon juice

BORDER FOLK FESTIVAL
EL PASO
Annual. September weekend.

6

A dab of background will help you enjoy your visit to the Border Folk Festival. In 1964 President Lyndon B. Johnson and Mexican President Adolfo L. Mateos unveiled a commemorative boundary marker at Chamizal. Today, Chamizal National Memorial continues to symbolize Mexican-American friendship and goodwill.

The Border Folk Festival calendar of events is lively, entertaining, and very, very busy. It's your opportunity to join in the excitement of traditional folk artists, entertainers, culinary experiences, and the all-around joyous sharing by different cultures from around the world . . . and the admission is free.

Although specific entertainers and attractions differ each year, here's a list to give you an idea of the event's enticing feasts and flavors. This event is renowned for its eclectic gathering of musicians, dancers, artisans, and culinary purveyors. Whether you go for the food, the entertainment, or the culture, you'll find a potpourri of ethnic and regional performers, storytellers in both English and Spanish, mariachi music, and Mexican folk dancers among the performers. During the festival you'll have the opportunity to watch artisans as they demonstrate how they create their works. Demonstrations include dulcimer building, horsehair hitching, rope tricks, woodworking, piñata making, and much more.

The entire community of El Paso, along with its neighbors from nearby cities, mark their calendars early and make plans to attend. One of the local attendees at the event said, "This is a marvelously full and fun celebration. There's so much to do it takes a day of running from place to place to see everything. It's one of my favorite events of the year." One can't deny that kind of endorsement.

You may want to diet a couple of days before attending. The wide range of culinary options includes ice cream treats, funnel cakes, bratwurst, gorditas, onion blossoms, turkey legs, churros, and roasted corn. Bet you can't eat just one!

Chamizal National Memorial is located in south-central El Paso, just north of the Rio Grande and immediately adjacent to the international boundary.

Southwestern Mushroom Pizza

4 6-inch flour tortillas

1 tablespoon vegetable oil

1 pound fresh white mushrooms,
sliced (about 5 cups)

$\frac{1}{2}$ cup sliced onion

$\frac{1}{2}$ cup thick, chunky salsa

1 cup shredded cooked chicken

$\frac{1}{2}$ cup shredded Monterey Jack
cheese

1 cup thinly sliced romaine or
iceberg lettuce

Preheat oven to 450°. Place tortillas on a baking sheet. Pierce surface with fork tines. Bake until crisp, 5 to 7 minutes. In a skillet, heat oil until hot, then add mushrooms and onions. Cook, stirring frequently, until liquid has evaporated and onion is tender, 6 to 8 minutes. Spread each tortilla with 2 tablespoons salsa, add mushroom mixture over salsa, top with chicken, and sprinkle with cheese. Bake until hot, 5 to 7 minutes. Top with lettuce.

Mushroom Council
Roseville, California

TACO SHELLS

To prepare a taco shell, fry 1 corn tortilla at a time in a half-inch of hot oil over high heat until it begins to blister and becomes limp. Fold in half and hold open with tongs so there is a space between for filling. Fry until crisp and light brown for a crisp taco, or fry until soft for a soft taco, turning as necessary. Drain well on paper towels. To keep shell warm until ready to fill, place on a paper-towel-lined pan in a 200° oven.

The Junior League of El Paso
Seasoned With Sun cookbook
El Paso, Texas

CHICKEN-FILLED TACOS

1 onion, finely chopped

1 small clove garlic, minced

6 tablespoons vegetable oil

4 ounces canned chopped green chilies, drained

1 teaspoon salt

$^{1}/_{2}$ teaspoon marjoram

14$^{1}/_{2}$ ounces canned whole tomatoes, drained

2 cups cooked and diced chicken

$^{1}/_{2}$ pint sour cream

1 can frozen or 1 cup fresh guacamole

12 prepared taco shells

1$^{1}/_{2}$ cups shredded Monterey Jack cheese

shredded lettuce

Sauté onion and garlic in oil until soft. Add chilies, salt, marjoram, and tomatoes. Break up tomatoes and cook mixture gently 10 minutes. Add chicken and cook slowly about 10 minutes or until chicken is heated thoroughly. Before filling prepared taco shells, drain chicken mixture. To assemble tacos, place 2 teaspoons chicken mixture, 2 teaspoons sour cream, and 2 teaspoons guacamole inside shells. Top with cheese and shredded lettuce.

The Junior League of El Paso
Seasoned With Sun cookbook
El Paso, Texas

Burritos

To prepare a burrito, heat flour tortilla briefly on a hot griddle or in the oven. Remove and lay tortilla flat. Spread with desired filling and fold sides over until tortilla is shaped like a tube. Hold together with a toothpick. Burritos may be served with picante sauce or taco sauce. Each person is usually served 2 burritos. They can be filled with any, or a combination of any, delicious Mexican treats such as chili con carne, refritos, chili con queso, guacamole, scrambled eggs with green chili, or leftover diced or shredded roast, fried with onions, potatoes, and green chili.

The Junior League of El Paso
Seasoned With Sun cookbook
El Paso, Texas

CHILI RELLENO SOUFFLÉ

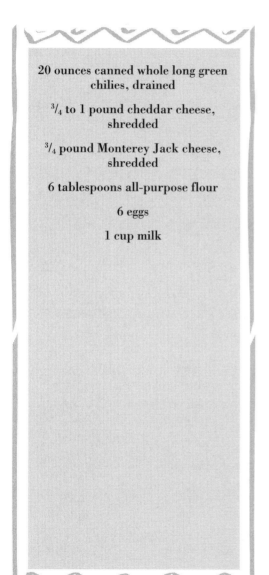

20 ounces canned whole long green
chilies, drained

3/4 to 1 pound cheddar cheese,
shredded

3/4 pound Monterey Jack cheese,
shredded

6 tablespoons all-purpose flour

6 eggs

1 cup milk

Preheat oven to 350°. Slit chilies open and wash out seeds. Dry well. Mix cheeses together. Spray a 9 x 3-inch baking dish with nonstick vegetable spray. Lay half the chilies in bottom of baking dish and cover with half the cheese mixture. Using sifter, sprinkle well with 3 tablespoons flour. Repeat layers, ending with flour. May be made 1 or 2 days ahead, and at this point, covered tightly with plastic wrap and refrigerated. Just before baking, beat eggs and milk together. Pour on top. Bake uncovered 30 minutes or until set.

The Junior League of El Paso
Seasoned with Sun cookbook
El Paso, Texas

 Excellent when served with tossed green or
fresh fruit salad and hard rolls.

BUTTERFIELD STAGE DAYS
BRIDGEPORT
Annual. July weekend. Dates vary.

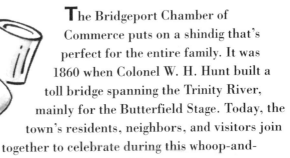

The Bridgeport Chamber of Commerce puts on a shindig that's perfect for the entire family. It was 1860 when Colonel W. H. Hunt built a toll bridge spanning the Trinity River, mainly for the Butterfield Stage. Today, the town's residents, neighbors, and visitors join together to celebrate during this whoop-and-holler weekend. You might as well plan to join in the fun. You won't be sorry.

Each year thousands of folks come to the event held in Harwood City Park and downtown Bridgeport. Many come for the fine victuals served during the Barbecue Cookout, but there's no lack of participants for the rest of the activities and programs. The Barbecue Cookout is served from 5 P.M. to 8 P.M. Saturday evening when buoyant chamber directors, members, and other volunteers cook and serve all the food. The lively action literally begins on Friday night when the folks gather at the park to prepare the meat, get it on the cookers, and then sit around telling tall tales and sharing a lot of fun and fellowship. It's a night of little sleep as the local "chefs" continue to monitor the progress of the briskets.

The next morning, with sleepy eyes and a growth of beard, the cooks are still enthusiastic. They oversee the day-long cooking of the beans in a specially built cooker. The justice of the peace cooks the chicken to perfection and others prepare the coleslaw. All this in time for the serving crew to arrive at about 3:30 P.M. to get the tables ready and put out the onions, jalapeño peppers, pickles, bread, and beverages. The cooks slice the meat, carry it to the tables on large trays, and the serving begins.

That's not all that happens during this hometown event. There are dazzling carnival rides for the young and the young at heart. Saturday activities begin with the children's parade at 9:30 A.M., followed by an arts-and-crafts sale, contests, tournaments, musical entertainment, and an antique and vintage car show. Youngsters are entertained with train, pony, and cart rides. Everyone hops aboard the free stagecoach rides available throughout the day, and the tempting smell of barbecue fills the Texas air.

The weekend following the cookout, Rodeo Arena is filled to capacity as the Bridgeport Riding Club provides three big nights of boisterous rodeo performances. The activities begin with a parade and end up at the arena for bareback and saddle-bronc riding, calf roping, steer wrestling, team roping, and more. For kids twelve and under, a calf scramble is held each night.

Bridgeport has a population of about 4,500 and is located 45 miles northwest of Fort Worth.

SOUTHWEST SIZZLIN' STEAKS

Mix all marinade ingredients. Brush over both sides of steaks, cover and refrigerate overnight. Spray 8-inch nonstick skillet with cooking spray. Sauté garlic, onion, green pepper, cumin, and oregano on moderate heat, stirring frequently, for 10 minutes. Add beans and 2 tablespoons water. Cover and cook 5 minutes on very low heat. Taste and add garlic salt to taste. Meanwhile, sear steaks in a heavy frying pan on medium heat. Sauté 5 minutes per side for medium-rare doneness. Check beans, adding 1 to 2 tablespoons water if necessary.

Texas Beef Council
Austin, Texas

 Serve steaks with beans and Pico de Gallo. (For Pico de Gallo recipe, see index.)

Marinade

1 teaspoon olive oil

2 tablespoons dry white wine

2 tablespoons light soy sauce

$1/8$ teaspoon hot pepper sauce

1 clove garlic, minced

Steaks

4 beef chuck steaks or rib-eye steaks, cut 1-inch thick

olive oil-flavored cooking spray

2 cloves garlic, minced

$1/2$ cup chopped onion

$1/4$ cup chopped green pepper

$1/2$ teaspoon cumin

$1/4$ teaspoon oregano

15 ounces canned black beans, drained

$1/4$ teaspoon garlic salt, to taste

TEXAS PECAN COUNTRY CHICKEN

4 boneless, skinless chicken breasts

$^3/_4$ teaspoon salt

$^1/_2$ teaspoon freshly ground pepper

8 ounces fresh mushrooms, chopped

$^1/_2$ small onion, diced, or 6 green onions, chopped

2 tablespoons butter

4 ounces cream cheese, softened

1 tablespoon French-style mustard

1 tablespoon snipped fresh thyme or 1 teaspoon dried thyme

$1^1/_2$ cups finely diced Texas pecans

1 cup finely diced bread crumbs

$^1/_4$ cup minced fresh parsley

$^1/_2$ cup butter, melted

On hard surface with meat mallet, pound chicken to $^1/_4$-inch thickness. Sprinkle with salt and pepper. Sauté mushrooms and onions in butter. Cool. Mix with cream cheese, mustard, and thyme. Divide into 4 equal portions and spread on each piece of chicken. Fold ends over and roll up, pressing edges to seal. Mix pecans, bread crumbs, and parsley in a bowl. Dip chicken in butter, then into crumbs, turning to coat. Place on greased baking sheet, seam side down. Bake at 350° for 35 minutes or until done. Serve with rice.

Texas Pecan Growers Association
College Station, Texas

CHICKEN OR TURKEY AND DUMPLINGS

Mix the flour and water in a pan until smooth, slowly stir in broth, cook and stir until thickened. Add chicken or turkey, salt, and pepper. Heat to boiling.

To prepare the Dumpling Dough: Mix together dry ingredients; stir in milk to make thick dough mixture. Drop dumpling dough from a tablespoon onto gently boiling mixture to make 8 dumplings. Cover pan tightly and cook slowly for 15 minutes without lifting lid.

U.S. Department of Agriculture
Washington, D.C.

 Try serving with fresh green beans and sliced peaches for a delicious home-style meal.

4 tablespoons flour

4 tablespoons water

2 cups chicken or turkey broth

2 cups boneless pieces of barbecued chicken or turkey

salt and pepper to taste

dumpling dough (recipe below)

Dumpling Dough
$^2/_3$ cup flour

1 teaspoon baking powder

$^1/_4$ teaspoon salt

4 tablespoons milk

BORDER BEEF AND RICE BAKE

2 4.4- to 6.8-ounce packages
Spanish seasoned rice mix

1 pound ground beef

1 medium onion, chopped

1¼ ounces taco seasoning mix

6 corn tortillas

29 ounces canned Mexican-style
stewed tomatoes*

2 cups shredded Mexican-style
cheese blend**

fresh cilantro, chopped for garnish

❧

*Substitute 29 ounces canned
stewed tomatoes plus 4 ounces
canned chopped green chilies for
Mexican-style, if desired.

**Substitute shredded Monterey
Jack cheese for Mexican-style, if
desired.

Prepare rice according to package directions. Heat large skillet over medium-high heat until hot. Add beef, onion, and seasoning mix. Cook 5 to 7 minutes, or until beef is brown and onion is tender. Remove from heat; drain fat.

Tear 3 corn tortillas into bite-size pieces and place on bottom of a non-metallic 13 x 9 x 2-inch dish. Add half of beef mixture, spreading evenly. Top with half of rice mixture, half of the tomatoes, and half of the cheese. Repeat layers, except cheese. Cover and bake in 400° oven for 15 minutes. Uncover, top with remaining cheese, and bake 10 minutes more or until cheese is melted. Garnish with cilantro.

U.S.A. Rice Council
Houston, TX

CHARRO DAYS

BROWNSVILLE

Annual. Late February.

To get you off on the right foot, the *Brownsville Herald* newspaper defines The Charro as a ". . . dashing horseman, hero of Mexican history, song and folklore . . . [who] . . . has always been a romantic figure, a lover of the open range, and . . . the beauty of his country." Is there any better reason to celebrate than to honor such a person?

Brownsville's unique location makes it Texas's southernmost city. Its location on the Rio Grande, across from Matamoros, Mexico, prompted organizers to begin an event that celebrates the people of both cities, their cultures, and their unique geographic location on the border between two nations. It's a place that honors creative culinary preparation and presentation.

Since 1938 the two cities have joined together during Charro Days to present a spectacular four-day costume fiesta that features parades, carnivals, music, dancing, and foods of this colorful two-nation region. The fiesta is so popular it has been featured in *National Geographic* and *Time* magazines. It has drawn the interest of travelers far and wide and earned recognition as one of the top 100 events in North America.

Come along and take a look at the authentic costumes, outstanding activities, and carnival-like atmosphere that make Charro Days so memorable.

If you love a parade and all the color and pageantry that go along with it, then you'll want to attend all three parades that kick off the event. The youth parade is held Thursday afternoon, the Twilight Parade takes place Friday evening, and the Grand

Parade steps off at 1 P.M. on Saturday. The parades take place along Elizabeth Street and spotlight floats, costumes, cultures, equestrian units, entertainers, and marching bands making their way along Brownsville's main downtown thoroughfare.

Professional entertainers take center stage and fill it with Tejano music, Ballet Folklorico dances, and a full spectrum of cultural and contemporary musical performances. A traditional outdoor charro rodeo emphasizes the Mexican vaquero and the American cowboy. It's a production that showcases traditional charro customs that set them apart from other horsemen.

Culinary experiences include about every taste sensation you can think of. Throughout the event you'll discover a plethora of cuisine to please your palate. Walk through food-vendor locations, local restaurants, and curbside food merchants and you'll be dazzled by the temptations. Whether you crave the finest in Mexican dishes or fast-food victuals, you're apt to have your culinary fantasies satisfied in Brownsville, Texas.

Brownsville lies along U.S. Highway 83/77 at the southern tip of Texas, 25 miles west of the Gulf of Mexico.

All recipes for this section were provided by the Brownsville Junior Service League and appear in their *Beneath the Palms* cookbook.

Huevos Rancheros

(Ranch-Style Eggs)

In small skillet, heat 2 tablespoons oil. Holding tortillas with tongs, dip one at a time in hot oil for 10 seconds or until limp. Line a 10 x 6 x 2-inch baking dish with tortillas; keep warm. In same skillet, cook garlic and onion until tender. Stir in tomatoes, chilies, and salt. Simmer uncovered for 10 minutes. Spoon mixture over tortillas. In large skillet, heat remaining oil. Carefully break eggs into skillet; sprinkle with salt and pepper. When whites are set and edges cooked, add water. Cover skillet and cook eggs to desired doneness. Carefully arrange cooked eggs over sauce in baking dish. Sprinkle with cheese and serve hot.

2 tablespoons vegetable oil

6 6-inch corn tortillas

2 cloves garlic, minced

$1/2$ cup chopped onion

3 large tomatoes, peeled, cored, chopped

4 ounces canned chopped green chilies

$1/4$ teaspoon salt

1 tablespoon vegetable oil

6 eggs

salt and pepper to taste

1 tablespoon water

1 cup shredded Monterey Jack cheese

ARROZ CON QUESO

(Rice with Cheese)

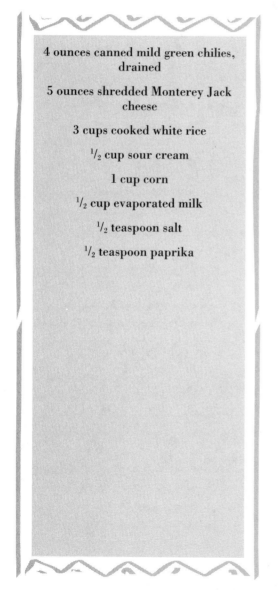

4 ounces canned mild green chilies, drained

5 ounces shredded Monterey Jack cheese

3 cups cooked white rice

$\frac{1}{2}$ cup sour cream

1 cup corn

$\frac{1}{2}$ cup evaporated milk

$\frac{1}{2}$ teaspoon salt

$\frac{1}{2}$ teaspoon paprika

Mix all ingredients, except 4 tablespoons cheese. Pour into a buttered 1-quart casserole dish. Top with reserved cheese. Bake at 350° for 30 minutes.

ENCHILADAS TAMPICO

Place tomatoes, chilies, coriander, and salt in a blender. Process until smooth. Add sour cream, blend and set aside. In skillet, melt margarine, sauté onion until transparent, add cream cheese and blend well. Stir in chicken. Soften flour tortillas in microwave about 30 seconds. Place equal amounts of chicken mixture in each tortilla and roll tightly; place seam side down in a 7 x 11-inch baking dish. Pour sauce over enchiladas. Cover; microwave on high for 7 minutes, rotating the dish once. Sprinkle cheese over top and microwave on high for an additional 3 minutes. Serve hot.

16 ounces canned tomatoes, drained

4 ounces canned whole green chilies, drained and seeded

$1/2$ teaspoon ground coriander

1 teaspoon salt

1 cup sour cream

1 teaspoon margarine

$1/4$ cup chopped onion

3 ounces packaged cream cheese, softened

2 cups chopped cooked chicken

12 flour tortillas

2 cups grated Monterey Jack cheese

MEXICAN RICE

1/4 cup bacon drippings

1 cup white rice

1 small onion, chopped

1 small bell pepper, cut into strips

1/2 cup stewed tomatoes

1 clove garlic, crushed

1 teaspoon salt

1/2 teaspoon freshly ground black pepper

10 3/4 ounces canned chicken broth

Heat bacon drippings, add rice, and brown slightly, stirring constantly. Add onion, pepper, tomatoes, and garlic. Cook until onion is translucent. Add remaining ingredients, stir once. Reduce heat to a simmer, cover and cook for 20 minutes without removing the cover. The dish is done when liquid has been absorbed.

CHILYMPIAD

SAN MARCOS

Annual. Third Friday and Saturday in September.

9

While there's some debate about where and when Texas's official state dish was first introduced—did it originate in a Spanish convent back in the 1600s or was it first developed by traveling cowboys in the 1800s—there's no question about where, how, and when the Republic of Texas Chilympiad got its start. A tasty Texas tradition since 1970, the event keeps getting hotter every year.

Friday's activities include the Texas State Collegiate Cookoff, games, giveaways, and the Miss Chilympiad Pageant, where each year the competition's intense as Texas beauties vie for the title of Miss Chilympiad and the Chili Court. You'll discover plenty of blue-jean hospitality and Texas tunes following the coronation and presentation of the winners.

Plan to stay up late, but set the alarm for early Saturday because the excitement begins at 8 A.M. The annual Run for the Red 5K run begins Saturday morning promptly, so get there an hour earlier to register in advance. The run will get your day off to a good start.

Saturday continues with the State Men's Championship Chili Cookoff headlining some of the world's finest chili competitors. It's claimed to be the largest chili cook-off in the world, with more than 450 cooking teams registering to participate in the annual festivities. It's said that the best time to sample chili at the cooks' booths is from 12:30 to 1:30 P.M. on Saturday. You'll want to get there early and stay late, though, to enjoy the many highlights and activities. The list of temptations is almost endless.

The Chilympiad gates open to the public at 9 A.M. Don't miss out on the beginning of the chili cook-off. While you're waiting for the teams and chefs to prepare their famous culinary temptations, you'll want to wander through the choice collection of arts and crafts and mosey over and appreciate the carnival, sandcastle construction, headliner entertainment, and some of the finest Harleys on earth displayed.

Chilympiad's cook-off remains an equal rights amendment supporter's nightmare—it's a men-only competition. Although mild protests against this sexist stand have been launched and words such as "chilibber" coined, the organizers have stuck to their guns. It's worthy of note, however, that there are two state women's cook-offs you'll want to attend. One is held in Sequin each spring and the other in Luckenback in the fall. Heck, it seems only right you make plans to visit them all!

San Marcos, home of this red-hot tradition, is located halfway between Austin and San Antonio on Interstate 35. The Hays County Civic Center is located about 1.5 miles south of San Marcos. Website address: www.axiom.net/chilympiad

DRUNKEN CHILI

Cut meat into bite-size pieces, brown, remove from pot and set aside. Pour out all but 2 tablespoons of grease, add onions, reduce heat slightly, and cook until onions start to turn translucent. Add garlic, tomatoes, chilies, and tomato sauce. Bring to a boil, reduce heat and simmer a few minutes. Return meat to pot, add 1 bottle of beer, and all spices, except masa harina. Cook for 1 to 2 hours over medium to low heat, stirring regularly. Mix masa harina in bowl with one-half bottle of beer until it becomes sludgy, adding more beer if too thick. Pour into pot and stir well. Add salt and pepper to taste. Serve with cornbread, crackers, or tostadas. If you must ruin it, sprinkle on cheese (that's a personal opinion). If you want to get run out of Texas, add a large can of chili beans.

Ray Finfer, Creator
Death by Chili
Irving, Texas

Chili is best cooked one day, refrigerated, and reheated later. It also freezes well and tastes even better when thawed and reheated.

4 to 6 pounds of meat (beef, venison, turkey

2 large white onions, chopped

4 cloves garlic, crushed

3 ripe tomatoes, seeded, chopped fine

2 to 3 serrano chilies, seeded, chopped

16 ounces canned tomato sauce

2 bottles Shiner Bock beer

4 tablespoons dark chili powder

2 teaspoons cumin seeds or powder

2 teaspoons ground oregano

2 teaspoons ground mustard

2 teaspoons red pepper flakes

1 teaspoon cayenne powder

2 teaspoons ground paprika

4 tablespoons masa harina

salt and pepper to taste

big pile of fresh grated cheddar cheese

HIKE 'N FIRE CHILI

2½ to 3 pounds chuck roast or tenders

5 to 6 drops of oil

1 large onion, diced

First Batch

1 tablespoon garlic

16 ounces canned tomato sauce

2 teaspoons paprika

1 teaspoon salt

16 ounces canned beef stock

2 teaspoons MSG

¼ teaspoon white pepper

Second Batch

1 tablespoon garlic

4 teaspoons cumin

¼ teaspoon oregano

¼ teaspoon white pepper

3 tablespoons dark chili powder

1 tablespoon light chili powder

4 teaspoons paprika

1 teaspoon salt

¼ teaspoon cayenne pepper

Cut meat into cubes. Add 5 to 6 drops of oil in skillet; when warm, add ⅓ meat, ⅓ onion, and sear. Do this 3 times in 3 batches. Put meat in chili pot. Simmer for 30 minutes, add first batch of ingredients, cook until meat is tender. Add second batch of ingredients and cook for 15 minutes.

Less Doss
Men's State Chilympiad Champion

GRAND PRIZE CHILI

In pot, place a little bit of oil and sear meat. Add tomato sauce, onion powder, paprika, cayenne pepper, bouillon cubes, and enough water to cover. Simmer for 1 1/2 hours. Add cumin, garlic powder, MSG, oregano, pepper, and chili powder. Correct with salt if needed. Cook an additional 30 minutes, or until meat is tender.

Ray Calhoun
Men's State Chilympiad Champion

3 pounds beef, cubed or coarse chili grind

1 teaspoon oil

8 ounces canned tomato sauce

1 tablespoon onion powder

1 tablespoon paprika

1 teaspoon cayenne pepper

2 small beef bouillon cubes

1 small chicken bouillon cube

1 teaspoon cumin

1 teaspoon garlic powder

1/2 teaspoon MSG, optional

1/2 teaspoon oregano

1/2 teaspoon black or white pepper

6 tablespoons chili powder

salt to taste

CITRUS FIESTA

MISSION

Annual. January or February.

Of all the colorful celebrations dotting the calendar of events in Texas each year, the Texas Citrus Fiesta is one of the few events in the state to have a historical marker dedicated to it for being one of the oldest. It was 1932 when a group of business people came up with an idea to pay tribute to the local citrus industry and Texas's own Ruby Red grapefruit. What resulted was a fiesta to let everyone nationwide in on the area's bountiful winter harvest of grapefruit and oranges.

Some people credit the lush subtropical climate of the lower Rio Grande Valley for the success of the citrus crops. Others ascribe the citrus success to the bold and determined perseverance of John H. Shary, known as the father of the Texas citrus industry. No doubt it's a combination of factors that today brings thousands of spectators and participants together in citrus celebration. Events take place in several locations around Mission, including the downtown area, Banworth Park, and Shary Golf Course.

Since the fiesta's founding, one of the prime features has been the showing off of lovely ladies and handsome young gentlemen at the Coronation of King Citrus and Queen Citrianna. More than a beauty pageant, the contest selects a royal couple who reigns over the weekend's festivities. The crowning takes place with a flourish of trumpets introducing the winners. Each year the crowns used are designed specifically for each new King and Queen.

You're bound to be impressed with the regalia of the royalty. Fresh cabbage, fern, and citrus leaves are part of the costumes. Using Rio Grande Valley citrus, vegetables, flowers, and foliage, designers make the breathtaking costumes in accordance with the fiesta's theme. The gowns have been exhibited at the Kennedy Center in Washington D.C., in Houston, and in Kansas City, Kansas. They also have been featured in *National Geographic* and *Southern Living* magazines.

The famous Parade of Oranges, one of the largest parades held in South Texas, is filled with musical entertainment and floats honoring the citrus industry. All the floats in the parade are covered with Rio Grande Valley products. The route is lined with more than 100,000 spectators who come to watch the colorful procession.

Additional happenings during the weekend include numerous educational booths, citrus exhibits, and arts-and-crafts displays. You'll be able to join in the fun and games at the Fiesta Fun Fair, Winter Texan events, live music, fun run, golf tournament, a carnival, and lively diversions for children. Entertainment includes dancers, folk dances, and plenty of musical performers.

Hungry? The Ranch Cook-Off offers a variety of food, including desserts, all cooked in Dutch ovens over a campfire. You'll be amazed at the fruit-filled creations lovingly prepared in an environment featuring authentic, restored, and antique covered wagons.

Mission advertises itself as "The Home of the Grapefruit." The next time you're strolling the aisles of a grocery store and run across a display of famed Texas Ruby Red grapefruit, you'll likely discover it's from the Mission area.

Mission is located off U.S. Highway 83 at the southeastern tip of Texas and alongside the Rio Grande.

TEXAS GRAPEFRUIT AND GULF SHRIMP SALAD

3 Ruby Red grapefruits, cut in half

1½ pounds cooked, cleaned shrimp

chilled salad greens

low-calorie French dressing

Remove grapefruit pieces carefully from halves and set aside. Remove all white membrane from grapefruit sections; clean each rind half. Line each rind with salad greens. Add shrimp to grapefruit sections. Spoon into grapefruit rinds lined with salad greens. Serve with low-calorie French dressing.

Melida Zapata
Mission, Texas

TEXAS FIESTA SALAD

Halve grapefruits, chill. In mixing bowl, whip cream with sugar, beat in sour cream. Fold in remaining ingredients. Cover and refrigerate. To serve, scoop salad onto Ruby Red grapefruit halves. Garnish with mint or watercress sprigs, if desired.

Francisco Jose Yanez
Mission, Texas

3 Ruby Red grapefruits

$1/_4$ cup whipping cream

1 tablespoon sugar

$1/_4$ cup sour cream

1 orange, peeled, cut up

1 small ripe banana, sliced

8 ounces canned crushed pineapple, drained

$1/_2$ cup miniature marshmallows

$1/_4$ cup shredded coconut

$1/_4$ cup chopped nuts

OLD-FASHIONED MUFFINS

2 TexaSweet red grapefruits

1 cup old-fashioned oats

$^1/_2$ cup butter or margarine

1 cup sugar

$^1/_2$ cup firmly packed brown sugar

2 eggs, beaten

1 cup all-purpose flour

1 teaspoon soda

$^1/_2$ teaspoon cinnamon

vanilla or fruit-flavored yogurt, or
whipped cream

Peel and section grapefruit over bowl, reserving juice. Set sections aside. Measure grapefruit juice, adding water to equal 1 $^1/_4$ cups liquid. Pour into a saucepan and bring to a boil. Remove from heat; and stir in oats and butter; let stand 20 minutes, covered. Combine remaining ingredients, except yogurt or whipped cream, in a mixing bowl. Stir in oats mixture, blending well. Pour into greased, 12-cup muffin pan. Bake at 350° for 15 to 20 minutes. Serve warm or cool; top with yogurt or whipped cream and grapefruit sections.

TexaSweet Citrus Marketing, Inc.
Mission, Texas

Texas Citrus Salsa

Peel, section, and dice grapefruit and orange. Combine all ingredients in a medium bowl. Drain juice before serving.

TexaSweet Citrus Marketing, Inc.
Mission, Texas

 This is excellent served as an appetizer or dip.

1 Texas red grapefruit

1 large Texas orange

1 medium tomato, chopped and seeded

1 cup diced green, red, and yellow bell pepper (use mixture for color)

1 jalapeño pepper, seeded, minced

3 tablespoons chopped red onion

1 tablespoon fresh chopped cilantro

$1^1/_2$ teaspoons sugar

$^1/_4$ teaspoon salt

CORN FESTIVAL
HOLLAND
Annual. Third Saturday in June.

The tiny town of Holland's friendly population swells as folks arrive from near and far to celebrate the town's heritage. It was 1877 when James R. Holland and his steam cotton gin settled a mile west of the original settlement along Darr's Creek. The Corn Festival was established as a bicentennial project for the city of Holland.

What you'll find is one heck of a friendly town and a spirited excuse for eating some mighty fine fixin's, applauding the parade participants, and dancin' in the streets. The schedule doesn't change much from year to year but that doesn't matter. "If it ain't broke, don't fix it!" certainly applies here. It all takes place in downtown Holland.

The day of the festival opens with the town parade of dignitaries, home-built floats, volunteer fire trucks, horses, and enough glittering fun to have this parade considered one of the largest in Central Texas. After the parade, a patriotic, flag-raising ceremony and the crowning of the Queen of the Corn Festival starts the celebration. Her majesty reigns over the entire event and takes part in various activities held throughout the year.

Competitions and contests take place in earnest early in the day, and you can sign up to join in at each of the events. There's always a corn-eating contest, the World Championship Corn Cob Throw, Corn Cob Relays, and the ever-popular Men, Women and Junior Corn Seed-Spitting contest. Afterwards you may want to try your hand at winning the Chicken-Flying Contest.

Other activities include the BBQ Cook-Off prepared by volunteers and friends of the Holland Volunteer Fire Department. The cook-off judging begins almost promptly at

3:00 P.M. Throughout the day, arts-and-crafts merchants line the area around the civic center and along the sidewalks. The street dance begins at 8:30 P.M.and you'll find yourself literally dancing in the streets following a day of fun and friendship.

Holland's fields of corn, churches, historical buildings, and annual events are found along Texas Highway 95 about 15 miles south of Temple.

CORN-HAM CASSEROLE

2 cups cooked, chopped ham, chicken, or beef

1½ cups cooked peas, drained

16 ounces canned cream-style corn

¼ pound processed American cheese, cubed

1 cup evaporated milk, divided

¼ cup chopped onion

1 tablespoon Worcestershire sauce

1 cup biscuit mix

½ cup cornmeal

2 tablespoons sugar

½ teaspoon salt

1 egg, beaten

Mix meat, peas, corn, cheese, ⅓ cup evaporated milk, onion, and Worcestershire sauce. Pour into greased 12 x 8-inch baking dish. Bake at 400° for 10 minutes or until mixture is bubbly around edges. Combine biscuit mix, cornmeal, sugar, salt, and beaten egg. Add remaining milk and mix well. Pour around edges of hot meat mixture, leaving center uncovered. Bake 20 minutes longer.

Barbara Hill
Holland, Texas

CORN AND SAUSAGE CASSEROLE

Combine corn, sausage, and green pepper; add seasonings. Place alternate layers of corn mixture, crumbs, and white sauce in 8½-inch square ovenproof casserole, topping with crumbs. Bake in 350° oven for about 30 minutes.

Mrs. A. C. Lindeman
Holland, Texas

2 cups fresh cut corn

1 can Vienna sausages, cut in thirds crosswise

½ cup chopped green pepper

½ teaspoon salt

dash of pepper

2 cups medium white sauce

1½ cups cracker or bread crumbs

CORN FRITTERS

1/2 cup flour

3/4 teaspoon baking powder

1/4 teaspoon salt

2 teaspoons sugar

1 egg

1/4 cup milk or water

1 tablespoon cooking oil

1 cup fresh or canned whole
kernel corn

Mix all ingredients in order of listing. Drop by tablespoon into fresh oil and deep-fry at 375° until golden brown.

Eunice Montgomery
Holland, Texas

There are many variations to making fritters; you can use cream, evaporated milk, or even water for the liquid. You can add chopped green pepper, shredded cheese, more or less corn, or any host of other flavors.

BEST ROASTED CORN EVER

Roast corn in husk on grill over glowing coals, turning often. Husk should be steaming hot in about 10 minutes and corn is ready to serve.

Roast corn in foil with husk on. Peel husk back to remove silk, brush with butter, sprinkle with seasoning, and replace husk. Wrap in foil, lay on grill over medium coals for about 25 minutes. Turn your corn frequently to avoid burning.

You can also remove the husk, brush the corn with butter and seasoning, double wrap in foil and roast for about 25 minutes, again turning frequently to avoid burning.

Terry Poland
Oxnard, California

COTTON PICKIN' FAIR & GO TEXAN DAYS

HILLSBORO
Annual. September.

12

According to organizers of the Cotton Pickin' Fair & Go Texan Days, the goal of the celebration is to remember and celebrate the agricultural roots of Hill Country. Held each year on the historic square in downtown Hillsboro, the event draws participants and visitors for a weekend of down-home cooking, antique farm equipment, arts and crafts, horseshoes, and hay hauling, plus much more.

Do you enjoy a relaxed, laid-back afternoon? You'll find you fit right in and look absolutely neighborly if you wear your jeans, boots, bolo tie, and top-of-the-line Stetson. Since the event celebrates Hillsboro's legacy as a top-rate producer of cotton, you'll find there's not much polyester around town.

What you will find located around the courthouse square are activities that include a barbecue cook-off sanctioned by the International Barbecue Cookers Association, plenty of classic cars, games of skill like dominoes and horseshoes, a plethora of antique farm equipment, and a wide variety of agricultural displays.

Affiliated with Go Texan Days, one of the featured events of the fair is the palate-perfect barbecue cook-off. The rules are set and participants must follow them in order to qualify for trophies and prize money. Teams participating in the delectable barbecue cook-off set up on Friday and the cooking excitement begins at 9 A.M. on Saturday. The cook-off has a guaranteed purse of $2,000, plus a jackpot bean category. Other categories include chicken, brisket, and spareribs.

Hillsboro folks are proud of their community and their cotton heritage. The whole town gets behind this rousing celebration. So get into your cotton duds, mosey on over, and join the singin', dancin', fiddlin', and eatin', in a town that celebrates its frontier traditions and farming heritage.

Hillsboro is located off Interstate 35 about 50 miles south of Fort Worth and Dallas.

BARBECUE BEEF MARINADE

2¹/₂ tablespoons brown sugar

2 tablespoons paprika

2 teaspoons dry mustard

2 teaspoons onion powder

2 teaspoons garlic powder

1 ¹/₂ teaspoons dried basil

1 teaspoon ground bay leaf

³/₄ teaspoon ground coriander

³/₄ teaspoon ground savory

³/₄ teaspoon dried thyme

³/₄ teaspoon ground black pepper

³/₄ teaspoon white pepper

¹/₈ teaspoon ground cumin

salt to taste

Combine all ingredients in small bowl. Store in an airtight container up to 4 months. To use the marinade, you need to massage it into the meat thoroughly the night before you plan to barbecue. Wrap meat in plastic and place in refrigerator until time to grill. The flavors are absorbed into the meat.

Texas Tom
Denton, Texas

CHILI WITH BEANS

Wash beans, cover to 2 inches above beans with water and soak in bowl overnight. Simmer, covered, in the same water until tender (approximately 2 hours.) Add tomatoes and simmer 5 minutes. Sauté green peppers slowly in salad oil for 5 minutes, add onion and cook until tender, stirring frequently. Add garlic and parsley. In a large skillet, melt butter and sauté beef and pork for 15 minutes. Add to the onion mixture, stir in chili powder, and cook 10 minutes. Add this mixture to beans and season with salt, pepper, and cumin; simmer, covered, for 1 hour. Remove lid and simmer 30 minutes longer. Skim fat off the top before serving.

Joseph Fessenden
Mission, Texas

$\frac{1}{2}$ pound dried pinto beans

2 28-ounce cans tomatoes

1 pound green bell peppers, diced

$1\frac{1}{2}$ tablespoons salad oil

$1\frac{1}{2}$ pounds onions, chopped

2 cloves garlic, crushed

$\frac{1}{2}$ cup fresh chopped parsley

1/2 cup butter

$2\frac{1}{2}$ pounds ground chuck

1 pound ground pork

$\frac{1}{2}$ cup chili powder (or to taste)

2 tablespoons salt (or to taste)

$1\frac{1}{2}$ teaspoons pepper (or to taste)

$1\frac{1}{2}$ teaspoons ground cumin

EYES ON TEXAS PORK BARBECUE

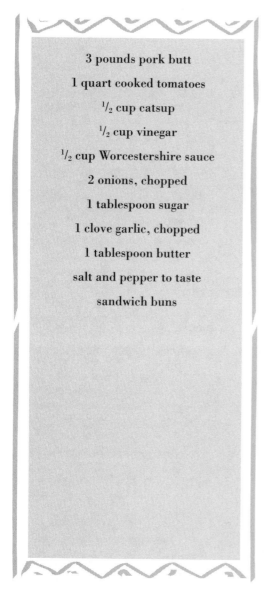

3 pounds pork butt

1 quart cooked tomatoes

¹/₂ cup catsup

¹/₂ cup vinegar

¹/₂ cup Worcestershire sauce

2 onions, chopped

1 tablespoon sugar

1 clove garlic, chopped

1 tablespoon butter

salt and pepper to taste

sandwich buns

Boil meat in water until tender. Pour off liquid and shred meat with 2 forks. Add all other ingredients and simmer until onions are tender. Serve on choice of sandwich buns.

Jim Sullivan
Laredo, Texas

 The Eyes of Texas Barbecue is an easy-to-make dish that's perfect served after a round-up.

CRAWFISH FESTIVAL
MAURICEVILLE
Annual. Third weekend in April.

The yearly Crawfish Festival gets underway on Friday night with the official "Grand Opening" ceremonies, entertainment, and evening dance. Topping the bill is the announcement of the winners of the Crawfish Festival Beauty Pageant. The Little Cypress-Mauriceville High School auditorium and grounds provide the weekend site for this rural, hometown celebration of the crawfish. It's not the grandest event held in Texas, but it's surely one of the tastiest and most good-natured.

Saturday's events begin with the Crawfish Festival Parade. It's your chance to watch the outcome of folks letting their imaginations run wild and coming up with a suitable "going country" theme, costume, float, or decorated car. It's a fun-filled festival parade that's bound to bring a smile to your face.

There's plenty of fun to keep you around long enough to work up an appetite for the tasty little crustacean that's closely related to the lobster. You'll discover all manner of crawfish dining options, but there's also shrimp-on-a-stick, alligator, funnel cakes, corn dogs, and more. In addition to the tasty crawfish, a barbecue and gumbo cook-off judging takes place on Sunday, so you'll no doubt want to spend another day in order to experience these additional dining options. You won't be sorry. It's hard to imagine missing out on any of these three days of family fun.

In case you need an excuse for delving heartily into the food, you might want to join in the numerous competitions and contests. You can select and race your entry in the crawfish races, fiercely toss around a few horseshoes, or join the lively competitors and their partners as they challenge one another on the obstacle course. It's not as easy as it might first appear. Contestants must run through tires, jump a four-foot hole, hop over hay bales, pick up a water balloon and deftly carry it to a table where they pick up an egg on a spoon and run back to home base, and hand it (unbroken) to a partner who continues to the finish line.

By then, you'll no doubt want to quietly stroll through the craft booths filled with homemade gift and food items. If you want more action, there are always plenty of carnival rides and attractions. Saturday afternoon brings everyone together to see who will be top bidder on dozens of donated items contributed to the auction.

Mauriceville lies about 7 miles southwest of Louisiana where Texas Highways 12 and 62 intersect.

All recipes for this section from Frugé's Cajun Crawfish Company, Crowley, LA 70526, 888-254-8626.

FRENCH-FRIED CRAWFISH

Heat oil to 375° in deep-fat fryer or kettle. Combine flour, salt, and pepper. Coat crawfish with flour mixture. Dip crawfish into beaten eggs, then coat with bread crumbs. Fry until golden brown. Serve with catsup or cocktail sauce.

oil for deep-frying

1/2 cup all-purpose flour

1 teaspoon salt

1/4 teaspoon red pepper

1 pound crawfish

2 eggs, beaten

1 cup dry bread crumbs

CRAWFISH ÉTOUFFÉE

⅓ cup oil

4 tablespoons butter

¼ cup flour

1 medium onion, chopped

2 cloves garlic, minced

2 to 3 stalks celery, chopped

1 small bell pepper, diced

28 ounces canned tomatoes

¼ cup beer

½ teaspoon basil

¼ teaspoon thyme

1 bay leaf

nutmeg to taste

freshly ground black pepper
to taste

sprinkle Cajun spice

1 pound crawfish, peeled

To make the roux, heat oil and butter in a heavy skillet until hot. Gradually stir in the flour and stir constantly until the mixture turns brown. Be careful you don't burn the roux. Sauté the onion, garlic, celery, and bell pepper in the roux for 5 minutes. Add the tomatoes, beer, basil, thyme, bay leaf, nutmeg, pepper, and Cajun spice. Bring to a boil, stirring constantly. Reduce heat and simmer for 15 minutes, or until it thickens to a sauce. Add crawfish, simmer for an additional 5 minutes, or until crawfish are cooked. Remove bay leaf and serve. You can use shrimp or lobster instead of crawfish.

For the inexperienced, making the roux can be tricky . . . Be certain to stir the roux constantly or it will burn. "You can't stir the roux too much." Cook roux until it turns dark brown.

According to the fine folks at Frugé's, Crawfish Étouffée is one of the most popular Cajun crawfish recipes.

CRAWFISH JAMBALAYA

Brown sausage in pan. Remove sausage, then add onion, green onion, and bell pepper to sausage drippings. Sauté until onions are soft. Add sausage to onions and sauté together for a minute or two. Add bouillon, onion soup, and tomato sauce. Pour mixture into Dutch oven, add butter, crawfish tails, and rice. Bake for 1 hour at 350°. Serve immediately.

1 pound hot sausage

$\frac{1}{2}$ cup chopped onion

$\frac{1}{2}$ cup chopped green onion

$\frac{1}{2}$ cup chopped bell pepper

14.5 ounces canned beef bouillon

10.5 ounces canned French onion soup

1 8-ounce can tomato sauce

1 stick butter or margarine, cut into tablespoon-size pieces

1 pound crawfish tails

2 cups uncooked Uncle Ben's Long Grain Rice

DAIRY FESTIVAL & ICE CREAM FREEZE-OFF

SULPHUR SPRINGS

Annual. Usually first weekend in June.

14

Have you ever sat on the porch hand-cranking ice cream on a warm summer evening? Or, as a child did you cherish the ditty that went something like this: "I scream, you scream, we all scream for ice cream!"? If so, here's a celebration you don't want to miss. If you're an ice cream lover who seeks to satisfy your cravings, be certain you make an annual culinary pilgrimage to Sulphur Springs to sample some savory creations.

Ice cream making and tasting contests are held in the Big Dip Division for anyone fifteen years of age and older. First- and second-place awards are also given in the Little Dip Division, for children ages six through fourteen. Entries are divided into age divisions and flavor categories. While many contestants vie for the awards, around Sulphur Springs there's a saying: "If you don't compete, come to eat." It's so much delicious fun you may want to both compete and eat.

For more than thirty-five years the folks in Sulphur Springs have honored the dairy families in this town of nearly 500 dairies with one of the creamiest festivals in all of Texas. In fact, it's so creamy they actually advertise the town as "Udderly Fantastic." That's the kind of people they are in Sulphur Springs. The town's motto, "Where the natives are friendly . . . It's like a whole udder country," isn't mere hype. It's true.

You're in for an action-packed weekend when you drop what you're doing and head toward Northeast Texas. During the weekend you can pet a cow, try your hand at milking one during the milking contest, or prepare your favorite ice cream and perhaps win a prize. On Friday night, there's a big street dance held on the historic downtown square.

Saturday's events begin with the downtown parade. It celebrates all things rural and hometown. Then the square becomes the site for a variety of arts-and-crafts merchants as they sell some of the best cow souvenirs and other delights. Have you ever wanted a cow apron, cow mailbox, cow birdhouse, or perhaps your own cow? Who knows, you're apt to find what you want during this day of mooooving experiences. Around the square you'll also find local antique merchants and shops selling their old-fashioned treasures.

Part of the day should be spent at the fabulous Southwest Dairy Center. Complete with silo, the center focuses on the historic and contemporary dairy life of this leading dairy county—one of the largest producers in Texas and the United States Exhibits recall early-day milk production, a 1930s kitchen scene, and an early barn.

Perhaps the most fun of all for the gourmands among us is the old-time soda fountain. Surrounded by items from an era past, you can luxuriate with a soda, malted milk, milk shake, or sundae among the nostalgia of an ice cream parlor atmosphere. Wouldn't you know it, to find out their hours you call 903-439-MILK.

How sweet it is in Sulphur Springs. You'll find the town, and a whole lot of cows, along Interstate 30 northeast of Dallas. Get a mooove on or you may miss all the fun! Website location: www.tourtexas.com/sulphursprings

All recipes for this section provided by the Sulphur Springs Tourism & Visitors Bureau.

PLAIN VANILLA ICE CREAM

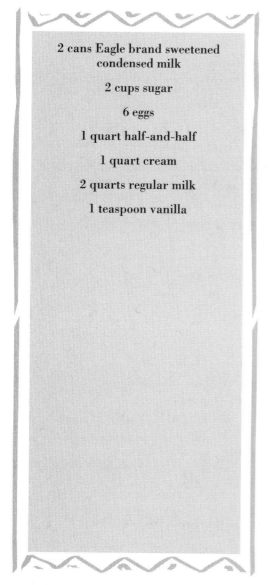

2 cans Eagle brand sweetened
condensed milk

2 cups sugar

6 eggs

1 quart half-and-half

1 quart cream

2 quarts regular milk

1 teaspoon vanilla

Mix all ingredients, freeze.

BANANA PUDDING ICE CREAM

Mix all ingredients, freeze.

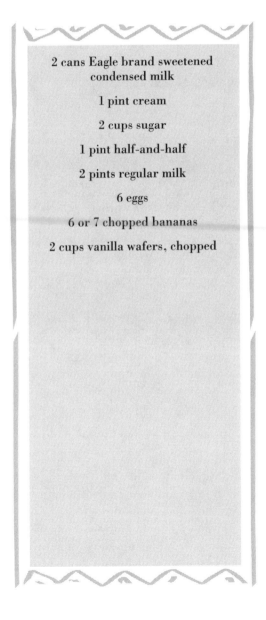

2 cans Eagle brand sweetened
condensed milk

1 pint cream

2 cups sugar

1 pint half-and-half

2 pints regular milk

6 eggs

6 or 7 chopped bananas

2 cups vanilla wafers, chopped

BUTTERFINGER ICE CREAM

2 cans sweetened condensed milk

2 milk cans of water

dash of salt

6 large eggs

2 tablespoons vanilla

2 pints whipping cream

1 Butterfinger candy bar, chopped

Mix condensed milk, water, and salt. Heat, stirring constantly. Beat eggs, add to milk mixture. Cook until thick. Remove from heat, cover, and chill. Stir in vanilla, cream, and Butterfinger. Freeze.

BANANA NUT ICE CREAM

Beat eggs, sugar, and salt. Heat milk over low heat, add egg mixture. Cook 5 minutes. Do not boil. Add Eagle brand milk; stir in cream, vanilla, mashed bananas, and nuts. Freeze.

6 eggs

2 cups sugar

dash salt

2 cups regular milk

1 can Eagle brand sweetened condensed milk

4 cups cream

$1\frac{1}{2}$ teaspoons vanilla

3 or 4 mashed bananas

$1\frac{1}{2}$ cups pecans, chopped

FALL FESTIVAL & WORLD CHAMPION STEW CONTEST

HOPKINS COUNTY

Annual. September dates vary.

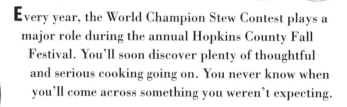

Every year, the World Champion Stew Contest plays a major role during the annual Hopkins County Fall Festival. You'll soon discover plenty of thoughtful and serious cooking going on. You never know when you'll come across something you weren't expecting.

The contest offers a multitude of taste delights for stew aficionados and participants. Dressed in imaginative and sometimes authentic costumes, chefs and their assistants assemble their decorated campsites and begin the campfires to the delight of shutterbugs diligently snapping their pictures.

At dawn, the rising wood smoke fills the air as the aroma of onions, garlic, and a variety of secret ingredients float across the festival grounds. You'll find yourself salivating as the 100 cooks, eager to please, begin to combine their ingredients in ten-gallon pots over the open fires. They're all hoping to win some of the several thousand dollars paid out to the best of hearty chicken, beef, and even squirrel stews cooked in huge cast-iron pots.

By 11 A.M. you can sample some oh-so-sublime stew from each of the stewpots as you walk through the campsites and mingle with cooks, judges, and other stew lovers. Then, as the activity winds down around the campfires, you can browse through arts-and-crafts booths, view the finals of the talent contest, cheer on the winners of the Cover Girl Awards, and enjoy a concert at the civic center.

If you're really lucky, you'll have several days to spend among the friendly people of Hopkins County during their annual week-long festival. Why not plan your vacation to take in the entire week that includes a pet show, a gospel songfest, tae kwon do demonstrations, a decorated doll contest, a fishing derby, and much more?

No matter what your schedule is, be certain you attend the World Champion Stew Contest held the last day of the Hopkins County Fall Festival.

The Hopkins County Fall Festival is held at the Regional Civic Center and Grounds in Sulphur Springs, situated on Interstate 30 between Dallas and Texarkana.

HOPKINS COUNTY STEW, FAMILY SIZE

2 pounds skinless chicken pieces

4 cups water

$^1/_2$ teaspoon salt

4 medium potatoes, diced

1 large onion, chopped

15 ounces canned tomato sauce

$14^1/_2$ ounces canned peeled diced tomatoes

1 teaspoon salt

1 teaspoon pepper

1 teaspoon chili powder

1 teaspoon paprika

15 ounces canned whole-kernel corn

15 ounces canned cream-style corn

Simmer first three ingredients in a 5-quart saucepan until chicken is tender. Reserving liquid, remove chicken pieces to be cooled, de-boned, and diced. Add potatoes and onion to liquid. If needed, add enough water to just cover these veggies and cook until potatoes are done. Add diced chicken, tomato sauce, diced tomatoes, salt, pepper, chili powder, and paprika. Bring to a boil. Add both cans of corn, stirring to prevent scorching. Reduce heat to simmer and cook for 15 minutes, stirring as needed. Add water if necessary.

World Champion Stew Contest Committee
Hopkins County, Texas

VEGETABLE STEW

Combine vegetables and bay leaf with chicken broth, bring to a boil, lower flame, and simmer 1 to $1\frac{1}{2}$ hours. Add seasonings to taste.

Mary Baumgartner
Hopkins County, Texas

1 small onion, chopped

2 carrots, chopped

1 zucchini, chopped

1 small potato, chopped

2 stalks celery, chopped

1 small can stewed tomatoes, chopped

1 bay leaf

$1\frac{1}{2}$ quarts chicken broth

seasonings to taste

PUEBLO GREEN CHILI STEW

2 pounds boneless pork sirloin or shoulder, cubed

1 tablespoon vegetable oil

36 ounces canned corn, drained

2 stalks celery, without leaves, diced

2 medium potatoes, diced

2 medium tomatoes, coarsely chopped

12 ounces canned diced green chilies

4 cups chicken broth

2 teaspoons ground cumin

1 teaspoon dried oregano

salt and pepper to taste

In a large Dutch oven or deep skillet with lid, sauté pork cubes in oil over medium-high heat until lightly browned. Add rest of ingredients to pot; cover and simmer for 1 hour. Serve hot with fresh corn or flour tortillas.

National Pork Producers Council
Des Moines, Iowa

TEXAS TENDERLOIN STEW

Trim fat from tenderloin. Combine flour, salt, marjoram, pepper, and MSG. With rim of saucer, pound this flour mixture into both sides of beef. Use rest of flour mixture to coat liver. Cut both pieces of meat into 2 x 1-inch strips. In hot butter, in a large skillet, sauté onions until golden; remove and reserve. In same butter, brown tenderloin and liver strips, turning them often. Add onions, water, and wine. Simmer, uncovered, over low heat, stirring occasionally until mixture is slightly thickened and meat is fork-tender, about 15 minutes. Meanwhile cook beans and peas 1 minute less than package directions and drain. Just before serving, gently stir them into stew. Serve with hot buttered noodles and crisp salad.

Bob Carter
Oxnard, California

Here's one of my favorite make-at-home stews for sharing with friends after a day of riding the freeways.

1 pound beef tenderloin, $^{1}/_{2}$-inch thick

3 tablespoons flour

2 teaspoons salt

$^{1}/_{2}$ teaspoon dried marjoram

$^{1}/_{4}$ teaspoon pepper

$^{1}/_{4}$ teaspoon MSG

$^{1}/_{2}$ pound calf liver, $^{1}/_{2}$-inch thick

$^{1}/_{4}$ cup butter or margarine

3 medium onions, thinly sliced

$^{3}/_{4}$ cup water

$^{1}/_{2}$ cup burgundy wine

9 ounces frozen cut green beans

10 ounces frozen green peas

FIERY FOODS SHOW
AUSTIN
Annual. August.

16

Considered the hottest weekend in Texas by many, the Fiery Foods event showcases the largest collection of hot and spicy products ever assembled in Texas. It's a perfect chance for foodies to subject their palates to some of the most diverse offerings of spicy foods ever displayed in the Lone Star State, as well as an opportunity to explore exotic and fascinating fiery foods from around the globe.

If your taste buds can take the heat, you'll want to sample carefully seasoned sauces, salsas, candies, honey, potato chips, pestos, nuts, jams, cactus, spices, sausages, soups, salad dressings, mustards, beans, catsup, and more. As one person told me, "It's kinda like your big toe in a hot bath. Indulge yourself slow and easy before you burn out."

You'll want to plan time at the Fiery Foods Cooking Stage to learn the latest culinary tips using chili peppers and fiery food products from many of the country's leading fiery foods chefs. There you'll also be able to talk about some of the recipes and preparations with top chefs from many restaurants and food manufacturing businesses.

Hey, go ahead and dress up yourself and your home in full chili pepper regalia. You'll find T-shirts, clothing, paintings, prints, kitchenware, and other accessories with a chili pepper flavor from the nation's top crafters.

Can you guess who sponsors the Hottest Media in Austin contest? Give up? It's a fun-filled and fiery competition sponsored by Tums (for the tummy)! Wouldn't you know? The event features radio, television, and newspaper personalities competing in a jalapeño-eating contest to win money for their favorite charity.

An area is set aside for those who love books and fine art. Stop by and you'll discover up-close and personal cookbooks and their authors along with artists exhibiting their hottest original creations and tasty limited-edition prints.

The capital city of Austin was named for Stephen F. Austin, the "Father of Texas." It's located off Interstate 35. The show's held at the Austin Convention Center, 500 E. Cesar Chavez.

SMOKY CHIPOTLE PESTO

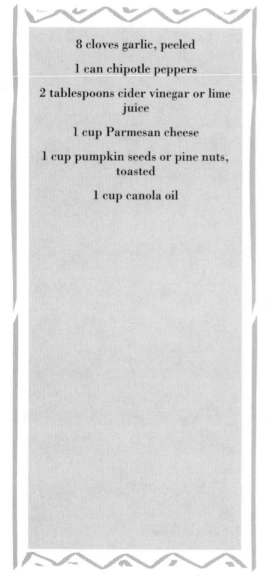

8 cloves garlic, peeled

1 can chipotle peppers

2 tablespoons cider vinegar or lime juice

1 cup Parmesan cheese

1 cup pumpkin seeds or pine nuts, toasted

1 cup canola oil

Chop garlic in food processor and add chipotle peppers and cider vinegar or lime juice; purée. Add Parmesan cheese and toasted seeds and chop fine. With processor running, drizzle in oil until pesto emulsifies and desired consistency is reached (you'll probably use less than 1 cup of oil). Use in quesadillas, baked potatoes, and pasta salads.

Chef J. P. Hayes
Sgt. Peppers
Austin, Texas

PUD THAI NOODLES

Soak rice sticks in lukewarm water until softened and drain through a strainer. In a large saucepan or wok, heat oil at medium heat, then stir-fry garlic until golden brown. Add shrimp or tofu and cabbage, stirring for 10 seconds. Turn to high heat and add the drained, softened rice sticks and the Pud Thai Sauce. Stir-fry until most of the sauce is absorbed by the mixture. Turn to medium heat and stir in the bean sprouts and scallions. Serve on a large serving plate garnished with freshly ground peanuts and paprika. Squeeze lime juice over freshly served portions.

Chef Foo Swasdee
Satay Restaurant
Austin, Texas

1 package Thai rice sticks
(1 to 3 mm.)

2 tablespoons canola oil

1 clove garlic, minced

1 cup shrimp, peeled, de-veined
(or fried tofu)

3 cups shredded green cabbage

8 ounces Satay's Original Pud Thai
Stir-Fry Sauce

3 cups bean sprouts

$1/4$ cup chopped scallions

3 tablespoons peanuts, freshly
ground, roasted

1 teaspoon paprika

4 to 5 wedges lime

GRILLED PORK LOIN

4 pounds boneless pork loin

1 jar Chef Valentine's Fiery
Jamaican Jerk Seasoning

Trim any excess fat from the loin roast. Cut the roast horizontally through the center. Using a kitchen fork, poke holes over the entire roast. Place the roast flat in a large dish. Rub jerk seasoning all over the roast, concentrating on the pricked holes. Cover and marinate for at least 4 hours, preferably overnight. Prepare grill until coals reach medium-hot heat and add wood chips or a sprig of fresh thyme. Place the pork on the grill with foil underneath it to catch the drippings. Cook over medium coals for approximately 2 hours or until a meat thermometer reads between 150 and 160°. The roast should be crisp on the outside and moist on the inside when done.

Chef Ron Valentine
Phoenix, Arizona

Chili Con Queso

Heat oil in 10-inch frying pan; sauté onion, pepper, and dry ingredients until onion is translucent. Add broth or water and let thicken. Add cheese and tomatoes. Carefully simmer for 5 to 10 minutes on low heat.

Matt Martinez, Jr.
Restaurant owner and cookbook author
Austin, Texas

1 tablespoon oil

$^1/_2$ onion, chopped

$^1/_2$ bell pepper or hot pepper, chopped

1 teaspoon cumin

1 teaspoon granulated garlic

$^1/_2$ teaspoon salt

2 tablespoons cornstarch

1 cup chicken broth or water

8 ounces cheddar cheese, shredded

1 cup chopped tomatoes

FOLKLIFE FESTIVAL
SAN ANTONIO
Annual. First weekend in August.

17

The Texas Folklife Festival is an annual, four-day cultural spectacular that celebrates the ethnic diversity, culinary traditions, and pioneer heritage of Texas. The event is sponsored by The University of Texas Institute of Texan Cultures.

Over forty ethnic and cultural groups participate each year and you'll get a glimpse into their unique lives and cultures. Each year brings new and diverse activities, and you're likely to experience things you'll find at no other event. At recent festivals visitors have been invited to:

make a one-eyed circular dog
shape a doll using corn husks
scratch a design on an egg
hand carve a calabash
learn the mystery of a magic amulet
carve a European whoopee stick
hold an antler
form a bluebonnet with strips of paper
make a bookmark out of horse hair

crack a cascaron on a friend
split an oak shingle
hand carve a rocking horse
create a wooden caricature
make a beaded bracelet
enlist in the military
perform a rope trick
become an honorary Texan
study onomastics

Come on now. You know you want to do them all. Here's the perfect time and place to experience each new adventure and skill.

The savory smells of herbs and spices of ethnic cuisine and other luscious foods fill the air. You can taste Alsatian parisa, German fleish salat, Belgian mussels, Czech klobasniks, Danish ableskiver, Greek koulourakia, Nigerian chin-chin, Norwegian smor brod, Spanish pepitos, and Filipino lumpia. All that and you don't even need your passport!

Between tastes you'll tap your toes and clap your hands as lively musicians sing and play, and ethnic dancers perform. For the little tykes there are festival animals to pet and a special Kids Day when kids get in free when accompanied by an adult.

In all, over 260 organizations and individuals representing about 100 countries and ethnic groups play a major role in the success of this premier festival. The Texas Folklife Festival is held on the grounds of HemisFair Park in downtown San Antonio. Website location: www.texancultures.utsa.edu/folklife.htm

MY MAMA'S CORNBREAD

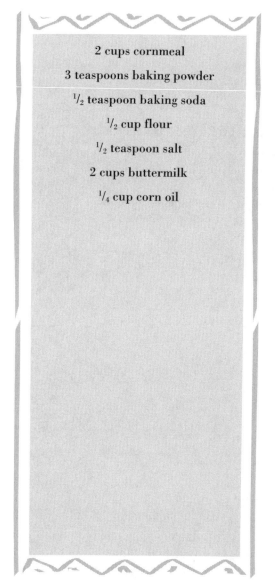

2 cups cornmeal

3 teaspoons baking powder

$^1/_2$ teaspoon baking soda

$^1/_2$ cup flour

$^1/_2$ teaspoon salt

2 cups buttermilk

$^1/_4$ cup corn oil

Combine all dry ingredients. Add buttermilk and corn oil, a small amount at a time, until mixed well and in a pouring consistency. Pour into a hot, well-greased, 9-inch iron skillet. Bake at 450° about 20 minutes.

Folklife Festival Committee
San Antonio, Texas

OLD FASHIONED HOT WATER CORNBREAD

Combine cornmeal and salt in a mixing bowl. Add water a little at a time and stir until meal sticks together. Moisten hands with water. Spoon mixture into hand and form into 6 patties approximately $\frac{1}{2}$-inch thick. Cook in hot oil in an iron skillet until brown on both sides. Serve hot with greens or any vegetable.

Folklife Festival Committee
San Antonio, Texas

1 cup cornmeal

$\frac{1}{4}$ teaspoon salt

1 cup boiling water

oil for cooking

SOURDOUGH BISCUITS

2 cups sifted flour

2 cups starter (recipe on next page)

$\frac{1}{2}$ teaspoon salt

1 tablespoon sugar

2 heaping teaspoons baking powder

3 tablespoons shortening

In a large bowl, form a nest or hollow in the sifted flour. Pour approximately 2 cups of "starter" into hollow. Add all other ingredients. Mix well to a soft dough. Pinch off in balls about the size of an egg and place in well-greased pans. Iron containers give best results. Grease tops of biscuits generously. Sourdough biscuits, like cowboys, need a rest, so at this point set them in a warm place to rise for 5 to 10 minutes before baking. It doesn't hurt to cover the biscuits while they're resting. Bake in a very hot oven until nicely browned. The closer the biscuits are crowded into the baking pan, the higher they will rise. Bake at 450° 12 to 15 minutes.

SOURDOUGH STARTER

Dissolve yeast in water. Add sugar, flour, and potato. Mix in crock and let rise for about 2 days until very light and slightly aged. Do not let mixture get too sour and do not let it chill.

One of the most important items in making and keeping sourdough starter going is a proper earthenware crock with a good lid, close-fitting, but not airtight. Do not use a tin container as the sourness of the dough will cause a poison. The size of the container will depend on the number of people you have to cook for and the amount of starter you wish to keep made up. For the above recipe, a 3-quart to 1-gallon crock is sufficient. If the container is too small, the starter will run out when it starts working.

To regenerate starter, add 1 cup warm water, 2 teaspoons sugar, and the amount of flour needed to mix to consistency of first starter. Set aside until biscuit time again. Never add yeast after the first time, but keep raw potato in starter all the time as food for the starter. Do not refrigerate starter. For best results your starter should be used daily.

Cliff Teinert
San Antonio, Texas

 Do not be discouraged if your first sourdough biscuits are not a howling success, as the starter improves with age.

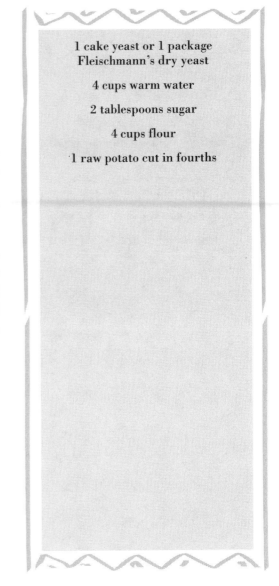

1 cake yeast or 1 package
Fleischmann's dry yeast

4 cups warm water

2 tablespoons sugar

4 cups flour

1 raw potato cut in fourths

NORWEGIAN GOULASH (LAPSKAUS)

2 pounds beef stew meat, cut up fine

¹/₂ pound lean salt pork, cut up

1¹/₂ cups chopped celery

2 white onions, chopped

4 medium potatoes, diced or sliced

carrots (optional)

salt and pepper to taste

2 tablespoons soy sauce (optional)

2²/₃ cups boiling water

In 2-quart iron pan, brown the meat and add celery, onions, potatoes, and carrots. Add remaining ingredients. Let simmer 1 hour or until meat is tender. Never boil, only simmer. Thicken gravy with a little flour if it appears too watery.

The Melting Pot: Ethnic Cuisine in Texas cookbook
University of Texas
Institute of Texan Cultures
San Antonio, Texas

GENERAL GRANBURY'S BIRTHDAY PARTY AND BEAN COOK-OFF

GRANBURY

Annual. Saturday in March.

18

For nearly twenty-five years, the folks in Granbury have celebrated the birthday of their namesake, General Hiram B. Granbury, a Confederate hero of the Civil War. Today it's a quaint historic city situated on the shores of Lake Granbury, just thirty minutes from Fort Worth. The birthday celebration takes place on the historic Granbury Texas Square.

The action gets underway as an eager audience anticipates the General Granbury Parade. It's the music and frivolity of a grand old hometown family parade. Participants and spectators fill the downtown historic square with excitement and enthusiasm as creatively decorated floats and entries vie for awards and prizes. Awards go to the best in a wide variety of categories, including commercial entry, decorated vehicle, riding unit, vintage vehicle, marching unit, and youth entry.

The day's outlandish events continue with the Outrageous Outhouse Race that claims to be unlike any race in the world. The rules are simple: All you need to do is build an outhouse, make a seat inside and a window, attach a push bar, and hold on. The race runs around Texas Square and requires one person to ride inside as the other pushes. At the halfway mark, participants switch places and the fun continues. The outhouse that crosses the line first, and is still in an upright position, wins the glory and awards.

Purveyors of food fill the spots around the north side of the courthouse and serve up platefuls of both traditional and unusual items such as hamburgers, hot dogs, bloomin' onions, spiral potatoes, barbecue, and fajitas. But be sure you leave room for the afternoon cook-off sampling. Nearby, talented and gifted vendors hawk their wares at more than sixty booths carrying a wide variety of handcrafted items. In fact, everything must be made by hand or it can't be sold.

As you'd expect, the big show takes place as the ladies and gentlemen take their places and the annual bean and rib cook-off gets under way. Organizers bill the cook-off as "A real gas!" Competition categories include red beans and ribs. The ribs may be pork or beef, but the beans have to be good ol' Texas red beans. Prize categories include "Best Beans," "Best Ribs," "Best Showmanship," and "People's Choice."

Granbury is located on U.S. Highway 377 and is served by Texas Highway 144 and roads 51 and 4.

Three of Granbury's historic bed-and-breakfast establishments share their favorite birthday recipes for this section.

EGGS O'HARA

In a large skillet, cook the bacon pieces until almost done, add the chopped onion, and cook until onion is translucent. Drain off all but about 2 tablespoons of the bacon fat. In a large bowl combine all other ingredients; mix well. Add to bacon/onion mixture in the pan and scramble until done. Serve hot.

Oak Tree Farm Bed and Breakfast
Granbury, Texas

1 pound bacon, cut across into
$\frac{1}{4}$-inch strips

1 large onion, chopped

1 dozen eggs

1 tablespoon chili sauce (like Heinz)

2 tablespoons Parmesan cheese,
grated

2 tablespoons chopped fresh parsley

2 or 3 good squirts Worcestershire
sauce

1 tablespoon water (or beer)

GRANNY NANNY'S PEANUT BUTTER PIE

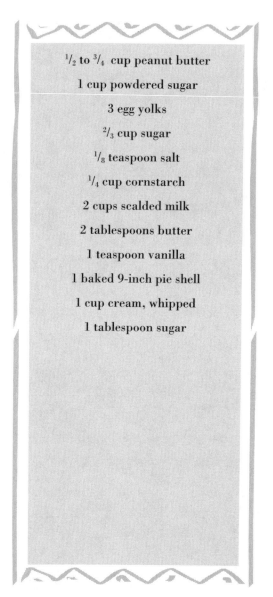

$^1/_2$ to $^3/_4$ cup peanut butter

1 cup powdered sugar

3 egg yolks

$^2/_3$ cup sugar

$^1/_8$ teaspoon salt

$^1/_4$ cup cornstarch

2 cups scalded milk

2 tablespoons butter

1 teaspoon vanilla

1 baked 9-inch pie shell

1 cup cream, whipped

1 tablespoon sugar

Blend the peanut butter and powdered sugar together in a small mixing bowl and set aside. Place egg yolks in the top of a double boiler; whip with electric mixer until fluffy. Combine sugar, salt, and cornstarch and beat into yolks. Add scalded milk and heat until smooth and thick, stirring constantly. Remove from heat, add butter and vanilla. Spread most of the peanut butter mixture in the bottom of baked pie shell (save a little for topping if desired). Pour hot custard over peanut butter and let cool. Add tablespoon of sugar to whipped cream. Top cooled pie with whipped cream and crumble remaining peanut butter mixture over top.

Julia Pannell
The Captain's House Historic Bed and Breakfast
Granbury, Texas

NICHOLS' MEXICALI GRITS

In a saucepan, bring the water to boiling and add the grits. Cook until grits are done, about 15 minutes. Remove from heat. Add remaining ingredients. Stir until cheese and butter are melted. Pour into an 8-inch square casserole dish or 8 individual baking cups (ramekins). Bake in 350° oven for 45 minutes, or until brown. Top with dab of mild picante sauce and sprinkle of shredded cheese.

Elizabeth Crockett Bed and Breakfast
Granbury, Texas

4 cups boiling water

1 cup old-fashioned grits

2 eggs, beaten

$^1/_2$ cup butter

10 ounces packaged Velveeta Mild Mexican cheese, cubed

1 teaspoon seasoning salt

fresh ground pepper to taste

mild picante sauce

sprinkle of shredded cheese

GENERAL SAM HOUSTON FOLK FESTIVAL

HUNTSVILLE

Annual. Third weekend in April.

There's no shortage of entertainment, demonstrations, or sensational cooking at this annual celebration of the life and times of General Sam Houston, legendary Texas hero. Houston played a leading and inspirational part in Texas's fight for independence and later served as president of the Republic of Texas, governor of the state, and United States senator.

Held at the Sam Houston Memorial Museum Complex, you'll get a glimpse of life in the 1800s as historical characters roam the festival grounds in authentic costumes and Citizen Soldiers of Texas recreate activities of the day. Cajun, Hispanic, African American, and American Indian groups share their heritage and food throughout this three-day folk festival. Entertainment includes theater performances, ethnic dancers, storytellers, and musicians. The event serves as a fund-raising effort for the museum.

Although the colorful combination of events changes each year, a look at past activities shows the scope and focus of each annual gathering. With all there is to see and do, you may have to visit the entire weekend in order to savor the rich and diverse activities available. Children's tents are set up with hands-on pioneer activities like candle making, stenciling, toy making, and game playing. Costumed demonstrators show their skills of broom and quilt making, weaving, glass blowing, woodcarving, and horsehair rope making.

Native American medicine men demonstrate nature's medicine chest of treatments and cures and lye soap makers tell how to make your own soap. Rugged and ragged members of the New Army of the Republic of Texas teach about the Texas Revolution and pioneer weapons.

The People of East Texas ethnic tents include African American culture with squirrel chowder, African sculpture, and American quilts. The Cajun culture tent includes accordian making and the smell of roux cooking. In the Mexican tent children try hitting a piñata and learn about the flavors of authentic Mexican foods. Additional food-tasting opportunities occur in the Grist Mill where a mechanical marvel grinds corn into meal and wheat into flour. At the Hearth Cooking area, with its reconstructed kitchen, visitors may sample authentically prepared treats.

Huntsville is located about 60 miles north of Houston on Interstate 45.

SHRIMP MANICOTTI FLORENTINE

10 manicotti shells

3 dozen large Shrimp, peeled and de-veined

2 tablespoons lemon juice

8 ounces frozen chopped spinach, thawed, well drained

1 can cream of mushroom soup

8 ounces sour cream

1 cup chopped onion

2 tablespoons butter or margarine

1 clove garlic, minced

$1/2$ teaspoon sweet basil

1 tablespoon dried chopped parsley

1 tablespoon black pepper

1 teaspoon salt

red pepper to taste

4 ounces canned sliced mushrooms, drained, except 1 tablespoon liquid

1 cup grated provolone cheese

Cook manicotti shells according to package; omit salt. Drain, rinse with cold water. Place on waxed paper to cool. Boil shrimp in water to which you have added the lemon juice. Boil 5 to 6 minutes. Rinse with cool water, chop coarsely, and mix with spinach. Mix soup and sour cream. Divide. Mix half with shrimp and spinach. Stuff shells with shrimp mixture and place in a well-greased 9 x 11-inch baking dish. Sauté onion in butter, add seasonings, mushrooms, and liquid. Stir in second half of soup and sour cream mixture. Spoon over manicotti shells. Bake at 350° for about 30 minutes or until thoroughly heated. Sprinkle with cheese and cook until melted.

Melina McGowen
Conroe Courier Holiday Cookbook First Place winner
Conroe, Texas

PICO DE GALLO

Mix all ingredients and chill. Serve with dip chips. To use as a sauce, put in a blender and purée.

Emily Avila
Mission, Texas

1 cup well-chopped onion

1 cup cilantro, well chopped

$\frac{1}{3}$ cup well-chopped jalapeño peppers

6 medium tomatoes, well chopped

juice of 1 lemon

salt to taste

COWBOY STEAK AND POTATOES

Marinade

2 tablespoons blue cheese

1 large clove garlic, chopped fine

1 teaspoon black pepper

1 teaspoon salt

1 tablespoon soy sauce

1 tablespoon Worcestershire sauce

1 heaping tablespoon powdered instant coffee

$1/4$ cup cooking oil

Steak and Potatoes

2 pounds top sirloin, cut 2 inches thick

8 medium red potatoes, cut into $1^1/_2$-inch wedges

oil to brush potatoes

1 package dried onion soup mix

vegetable cooking spray

Mix marinade ingredients in food processor or blender. Pour over steak and rub into the surface. Marinate steak several hours or overnight in the refrigerator. To prepare potatoes, brush with oil and coat with onion soup mix. Spray rack of broiler pan with vegetable cooking spray. Place steak and potatoes on rack and broil 6 inches from the heat. Cook for 30 minutes until steaks are medium rare and potatoes are tender, turning once. Carve steak across grain into thin slices. Serve with red potatoes.

Texas Beef Council
Austin, Texas

SPANISH PORK CASSEROLE

Place beans, undrained tomatoes, rice and seasoning packet, onion, bell pepper, olives, water, garlic, and pepper in 5-quart slow cooker. Mix until well combined. Place pork over mixture. Cover, cook on low heat setting 4 hours, or until pork and rice are tender. Rice will become mushy if overcooked.

National Pork Producers Council
Des Moines, Iowa

$15^{1}/_{2}$ ounces canned garbanzo beans, drained

$14^{1}/_{2}$ ounces canned Mexican-style stewed tomatoes, undrained

6.8 ounces packaged Spanish rice mix with seasoning packet

1 large onion, halved, thinly sliced

1 red bell pepper, cut into $2 \times {}^{1}/_{4}$-inch strips

1 cup halved pimento-stuffed green olives, drained

$^{1}/_{3}$ cup water

1 clove garlic, minced

$^{1}/_{8}$ teaspoon pepper

$1^{1}/_{2}$ pounds boneless pork loin, cut into 1-inch cubes

GERMANFEST
MUENSTER
Annual. Last full weekend in April.

20

What's more appropriate than a Germanfest in a community where most of the population of 1,700 are descendants of German settlers? Sponsored by the Chamber of Commerce and several corporate leaders, Germanfest begins with a hearty *Willkommen* on Friday and continues throughout the weekend. The three-day event attracts thousands of celebrants. Be sure you bring a *guten apetit* because you'll be tempted by such taste treats as German sausage, scrumptious apple strudel, hearty cheeses, and homemade breads, cakes, and pies. Here's your chance to experience a delightful weekend of family food, fun, and frolic.

During Germanfest, the North Texas BBQ Cook-Off participants begin their preparations early Friday evening and continue through Sunday when the trophies and cash prizes are presented and foodies savor the delicious results. Cooking competitions include chili, sausage, ribs, and brisket all cooked up in surprising fashions. Everyone is eligible to enter, so why not join in this culinary adventure with your personal recipe favorite?

Other special activities open to the public include a 5K and 15K Germanfest Fun Run, Metric Century Bicycle Rally, the North Texas Championship Arm Wrestling Contest, 11K Volksmarch, and the Sausage and Rib Cook-Off. Everyone is welcome to join the action. You can pick up a Bicycle Rally start card on Saturday morning. The rally travels over paved roads and along scenic highways. You can stretch your muscles and give them an amazing athletic workout during the arm wrestling events.

Two stages feature lavish family entertainment including dancing, music, mimes, magicians, clowns, and storytellers. There's the Karneval and Kinder Theater for kids, and everyone delights in the folk dancing.

The main Germanfest activities take place at City Park with bicycle and running events occurring throughout the community.

Muenster is situated on U.S. Highway 82, 14 miles west of Interstate 35 and 70 miles east of Wichita Falls.

APFELSTRUDEL

Pastry
3¼ cups sifted flour

pinch of salt

2 tablespoons shortening

2 eggs

1 tablespoon melted butter

2 tablespoons sour cream

lukewarm water

Apple Filling
6 apples, sliced

2 tablespoons lemon juice

½ cup raisins

½ cup chopped pecans

½ cup sugar

½ teaspoon cinnamon

1 tablespoon flour

Glaze
1 egg yolk

1 tablespoon sour cream

2 tablespoons sugar

powdered sugar for topping

Mix flour, salt, and shortening. Combine eggs, melted butter, and sour cream with dry mixture; add enough lukewarm water to make a soft but firm dough. Knead for 15 to 20 minutes or until dough is elastic and bubbles on surface. Cover and set in warm place for 30 minutes. Combine apples, lemon juice, raisins, pecans, sugar, cinnamon, and flour; set aside. Beat egg yolk, blend in sour cream and sugar; set aside.

Place a large, clean cloth over a large table, sprinkle with additional flour, and place dough in center. Roll dough, lift, pull, and stretch carefully into a rectangular shape until dough is as thin as paper. Trim edges. Brush with butter and spread apple filling over surface to within 1½ inches of one end; roll up into a long thin roll. Carefully place on a well-greased baking sheet, twisting to fit pan. Brush with glaze. Place strudel in preheated 400° oven and bake 20 to 25 minutes or until golden brown. Sprinkle with powdered sugar, cut into thick slices, and serve with a scoop of ice cream if desired.

Margie Starke
Muenster, Texas

BAYERISCHES KRAUT

Warm oil in large skillet and add onion. Stir until onion is glazed. Add grated cabbage. Do not brown. Add caraway seeds and salt lightly. Add very little water to make steam. Cover and cook for about $1/2$ hour.

Muenster Chamber of Commerce
Muenster, Texas

$1^1/_2$ tablespoons oil

1 small onion, chopped

1 large head white cabbage, grated

2 teaspoons caraway seeds

salt to taste

POLISH-STYLE SCHNITZEL

6 boneless pork loin cutlets, trimmed
(about 2 pounds)

$1/2$ cup all-purpose flour

2 teaspoons seasoned salt

$1/2$ teaspoon freshly ground pepper

2 eggs

$1/4$ cup milk

$1 1/2$ cups fresh bread crumbs

2 teaspoons paprika

6 tablespoons solid vegetable
shortening

2 tablespoons all-purpose flour

$1/2$ teaspoon dried dill

$1 1/2$ cups chicken broth

1 cup sour cream, room temperature

Place cutlets between 2 sheets of waxed paper and flatten to $1/4$- to $1/2$-inch thickness. Cut small slits around edges of pork to prevent curling. Set aside. Combine $1/2$ cup flour, salt, and pepper in shallow bowl or on sheet of waxed paper. Beat eggs with milk in another shallow bowl. Mix crumbs and paprika in small bowl or on another sheet of wax paper.

Put 3 tablespoons shortening in large skillet over medium heat. Dip cutlets in flour, then into egg mixture; coat with crumbs, covering completely. Add 3 cutlets to skillet and sauté 3 to 5 minutes per side. Transfer to platter and keep warm. Repeat process with remaining shortening and cutlets. Combine remaining flour with dill. Add to skillet, scraping up any browned bits clinging to the bottom of the pan. Add broth, stirring constantly until well blended. Stir in sour cream and cook until heated through. Spoon over cutlets or pass separately.

Richard J. Sepanski
Muenster, Texas

GERMAN RED CABBAGE

Heat the bacon grease in a large skillet or pot. Add the onion and sauté to soften, but do not brown. Add cabbage, stir well to coat all the cabbage with onion mixture. Cover tightly and let steam over low heat for 15 minutes. Add the rest of the ingredients and stir well. Let steam, tightly covered, over very low heat for 30 to 45 minutes. Test for taste and tenderness. May be served at tender-crisp point or cooked longer for softer cabbage.

Imogene Zimmerer
Muenster, Texas

$1/4$ cup bacon grease

1 large onion, chopped

2 pounds red cabbage, shredded

1 apple peeled and diced or $1/2$ cup applesauce

$1/4$ cup sugar

$1/4$ cup cider vinegar

$1/4$ cup dry white wine

$1^1/_2$ teaspoons salt

$1/4$ teaspoon pepper

HILL COUNTRY WINE & FOOD FESTIVAL

AUSTIN

Annual. Four days in April.

21

You can always plan on experiencing a true adventure in fine wine and unforgettable food during the Hill Country Wine & Food Festival. Each year thousands of wine and food connoisseurs gather to celebrate one of the nation's outstanding events.

Although many of the festival activities are held in the capital city of Austin, some events occur at wineries located throughout Texas Hill Country. As with all great events, the program is subject to minor changes each year.

A quick look at previous programs validates the diversity of options available during the four-day celebration. An amazing array of seminars, tastings, and cooking school-sponsored workshops takes place. Food and wine lovers gather to discuss trends, participate in workshops, and enjoy some of the best food and wine from Texas and around the world.

Thursday's events commence with "Lunch in the Wine Country." In the beauty of the Texas Hill Country, you'll dine with Texas winemakers and enjoy their award-winning wines paired with exquisite cuisine by Texas chefs. Following lunch, buses transport festival goers to tastings held at a variety of wineries. The evening's dinner honors the Texas Hill Country Wine & Food Foundation.

Friday's activities generally include the first of the cooking programs and demonstrations, along with several seminars focusing on culinary skills and the finer points of wine making. It's during these sessions that you'll learn objective criteria to help you evaluate wine. You'll also experience firsthand food preparation, techniques, and tips. A fine wine charity auction usually ends Friday's activities.

The auction features many remarkable and unusual lots from around the world, including fine European and California vintages.

Saturday's events start with a champagne breakfast followed by seminars. The Winemakers Luncheon offers festival goers a chance to sample lunches from one of several downtown Austin restaurants. The centerpiece event of the entire festival is the Saturday night dinner highlighted by guest appearances and cooking by some of the world's most noted chefs. Celebrity guests come from top restaurants whose names are synonymous with the finest in American food and wine.

Sunday's major attraction is the "Wine & Food Fair." There you'll meet noted authors and sample tastings of Texas food and beverage products. Recent feature presentations have included "Serious Salsas," "Taking the Wild Out of Texas Game," "Bock Battered Quail," "Chocolate Creations," and "Wine for a Healthy Heart." Special attractions on Sunday may include the Texas Beef Council's authentic chuck wagon fixin's, wine and beer brewing tents, fresh and organic produce presentations by the Texas Department of Agriculture, and more.

Recipes for this section provided by René Bajeux, Executive Chef at the helm of the Windsor Court Hotel's Grill Room in New Orleans.

ALLIGATOR RAGOUT WITH CHIPOLTE CREOLE TOMATO SAUCE

$^1/_8$ cup extra virgin olive oil

$^1/_2$ cup chopped leeks (white and green parts)

$^1/_2$ cup diced onion

2 pounds alligator meat (tenderized), diced to $^1/_4$-inch cubes

$^1/_8$ teaspoon salt, or to taste

$^1/_8$ teaspoon pepper, or to taste

1 tablespoon chopped garlic

$^3/_4$ cup peeled, diced tomatoes

zest of 2 oranges

$^1/_4$ cup diced Andouille sausage

$^1/_4$ cup diced, roasted chipotle pepper

1 cup white wine

2 cups chicken stock

1 tablespoon butter

1 tablespoon flour

1 cup corn

Place olive oil in medium-size stockpot over medium heat. Add leeks and onion, cook until tender and slightly browned. Add alligator meat. Add salt, pepper, garlic, tomatoes, and orange zest. Cook 3 minutes. Add sausage and chipotle pepper. Deglaze with white wine. Add chicken stock and bring to a boil.

Melt butter in a small sauté pan over low heat. Add flour and stir continuously 1$^1/_2$ to 2 minutes or until flour is cooked. Add 1 cup hot chicken stock mixture to roux, whisking to remove lumps. Immediately add back into stockpot and simmer until mixture begins to thicken. Add corn; let mixture stew up to 1 hour. Serve with rice or pasta.

TUNA ENCRUSTED WITH HERBS RATATOUILLE RISOTTO, SAFFRON AIOLI, AND MERLOT JUS

Cut the tuna into four 8-ounce blocks. Brush with ¼ cup olive oil and roll in basil, parsley, cilantro, and thyme. Refrigerate until ready to grill.

Risotto: place ¼ cup olive oil in large stock pot over medium heat. Add onion and sauté until transparent. Add red bell pepper, eggplant, zucchini, and tomato. Add rice, 2 cups chicken stock, and garlic. Stir rice frequently, add remaining chicken stock, as needed, until liquid is absorbed and risotto is tender and cooked.

Aioli: Place garlic and egg yolks in blender, purée until smooth. Add lemon juice and saffron. Gradually add ⅛ cup olive oil. Cover and refrigerate until ready to serve.

Merlot jus: Place ⅛ cup olive oil in sauté pan over medium heat. Add shallots and sauté until tender. Add red wine and reduce until syrupy. Add veal stock and cassis liqueur. Reduce heat to low and cook 10 minutes. In small bowl combine cornstarch and water, stirring to dissolve. Add cornstarch to shallot mixture, stirring constantly; cook until thickened to desired consistency.

Grill tuna on all sides to cook rare or medium rare. Slice tuna into 8 pieces. Place risotto in center of plate, arrange tuna around it. Drizzle tuna with merlot. Spoon saffron aioli around the tuna. Garnish with julienned beets.

Tuna
2 pounds fresh tuna
¼ cup extra virgin olive oil
¼ cup finely chopped basil
¼ cup finely chopped parsley
¼ cup finely chopped cilantro
¼ cup finely chopped thyme

Risotto
¼ cup extra virgin olive oil
¼ cup diced onion
¼ cup diced red bell pepper
¼ cup peeled, diced eggplant
¼ cup diced zucchini
¼ cup diced, peeled, seeded tomato
2 cups uncooked rice
1 quart chicken stock, warmed
1 teaspoon minced garlic

Aioli
1 tablespoon puréed garlic, or to taste
2 egg yolks
1 tablespoon lemon juice
⅛ teaspoon saffron
⅛ cup extra virgin olive oil, more if needed for desired consistency

Merlot Jus
⅛ cup extra virgin olive oil
⅛ cup chopped shallots
¼ cup red wine
2 cups veal stock
⅛ cup cassis liqueur
1½ tablespoons cornstarch
1½ to 2 tablespoons water
1 cup julienned fresh whole uncooked beets

Spring Roll of Louisiana Shrimp with Spicy Plum Sauce

Spring Rolls
1 teaspoon sesame oil

1 pound medium (31 to 35 size) shrimp, peeled, deveined

1/8 cup julienned carrots

1/3 cup julienned napa cabbage

1/8 cup julienned snow peas

4 cloves garlic, finely chopped

2 teaspoons chopped cilantro

1/8 teaspoon salt

1/8 teaspoon pepper

16 spring roll wrappers

2 egg whites

4 to 6 cups oil for deep-frying

8 sprigs cilantro

Spicy Plum Sauce
1 teaspoon sesame oil

3 teaspoons finely chopped onion

1/2 pound fresh plums, pitted, sliced

1/8 cup port wine

1 teaspoon Tabasco sauce

Spring Roll filling: Place sesame oil in sauté pan over medium-high heat. Add shrimp; sauté 3 minutes. Add carrots, cabbage, snow peas, garlic, and cilantro; sauté another 2 minutes. Season with salt and pepper. Place in refrigerator until cool, then divide and place the mixture in the center of each wrapper. Brush egg whites on all four edges. Fold two opposite corners together and seal. Then fold the other two opposite corners and seal. Refrigerate until ready to use.

Spicy Plum Sauce: Place sesame oil in sauté pan over medium heat. Add onion; sauté until lightly brown. Add plums, port wine, and Tabasco sauce. Reduce heat to low and cook 8 minutes, stirring frequently. Keep at room temperature until ready to serve.

Deep-fry spring rolls in hot oil 5 minutes. Slice diagonally. Garnish with a dollop of plum sauce and a sprig of cilantro. Yields 8 servings.

HOMINY GRITS CAKE WITH CRAWFISH RAGOUT

Cook grits in boiling water according to directions on package. Set aside. Place 1¼ tablespoons olive oil in skillet over medium heat. Add red bell pepper, yellow bell pepper, onion, and garlic; sauté until tender. Fold into grits. Cool to room temperature, cover; refrigerate 1 hour. Form 8 large individual patties out of cooled grits mixture. Set aside. Place 1 tablespoon olive oil in skillet, add Tasso ham; sauté over medium heat 1 minute. Add cream, basil, and habanero pepper; mix well. Add crawfish; cook for 3 minutes. Add salt and pepper. Place remaining olive oil in separate large skillet or sauté pan over medium heat. Brown cakes on both sides until lightly browned and crispy. Place 1 cake on each of 8 serving plates; spoon crawfish mixture over top. Garnish with basil leaf.

6 cups cooked grits

¼ cup extra virgin olive oil

¼ cup diced red bell pepper

¼ cup diced yellow bell pepper

¼ cup diced onion

3 tablespoons chopped garlic

⅛ cup diced Tasso ham

1 cup heavy whipping cream

1½ tablespoons chopped basil

1 teaspoon chopped habanero pepper

2 pounds fresh crawfish meat

⅛ teaspoon salt

⅛ teaspoon pepper

8 basil leaves for garnish

INTERNATIONAL APPLE FESTIVAL

MEDINA

Annual. Last Saturday in July.

22

If you've ever felt like experiencing a small-town festival, here's one that might fit the bill. It's filled with fresh-off-the-tree apples that are just right for cookin' and bakin'. You'll be able to pick what you want whether it's a single apple to chomp or a full truckload to carry back home for canning.

Picked at the peak of freshness, Texas apples make some of the best apple cider available around these parts. There's plenty of action throughout the day to test your skills and whet your appetite. Both adults and youngsters will find bobbin' for apples to their liking. The apple goodies are seemingly endless, and you can take your pick from a wide variety of apple-based taste treats.

When it's time to take a break from the apple crop, why not try your hand at shooting a musket or bow during the black powder and archery contests? Or, if it's more to your liking, browse through arts-and-crafts booths, and tap your feet and clap your hands as entertainers from three stages provide continuous live music and entertainment.

Kids will love the clowns, puppets, and games of skill at this annual shindig. After all, it's said that nothing comes close to the sweetness and taste of fresh-picked apples and the joy and excitement of a family festival.

Medina lies about 35 miles—as the crow flies—west of San Antonio along Highway 173. Watch for the apple farms and the friendly folks. You'll discover that the Medina River flows right through the festival grounds.

LOVE CREEK'S SPICY CIDER SYRUP

Combine cider, cinnamon (broken into pieces), and cloves. Cover and simmer 10 minutes. Strain. Combine cider, sugar, and corn syrup. Bring to a boil and boil briskly for 4 to 6 minutes. Cool slightly to serve on pancakes.

International Apple Festival
Medina, Texas

1 cup Love Creek Apple Cider

2 sticks cinnamon

12 whole cloves

$1/2$ cup sugar

2 tablespoons light corn syrup

LOVE CREEK'S APPLE-CHICKEN SALAD

Sauce

1 cup Hellmann's mayonnaise

4 ounces Love Creek Apple Chutney

1 teaspoon curry powder

2 teaspoons grated fresh lime peel

$1/4$ cup fresh lime juice

$1/2$ teaspoon salt

pepper to taste

Salad

2 Love Creek apples, cubed

2 cups chopped celery

$1/4$ cup chopped toasted salty pecans

4 cups cubed cooked white chicken meat

fresh garlic chives, to sprinkle on top

Sauce: Mix all ingredients together, cover and chill. Best to chill overnight.

Salad: Mix all salad ingredients together and pour sauce over mixture. Mix well, garnish with chives, and serve chilled.

International Apple Festival
Medina, Texas

MEDINA APPLE PIE

Preheat oven to 400°. Sprinkle apples with lemon juice. Combine sugar, flour, cinnamon, nutmeg, and salt. Mix with apples. Line a 9-inch pie pan with pastry. Fill with apple mixture and dot with butter. Put on top crust, cutting slits for steam to escape. Seal edges; sprinkle with sugar. Bake for 50 minutes. Serve warm or cool.

International Apple Festival
Medina, Texas

6 to 8 tart Texas apples, peeled, cored and thinly sliced (6 cups)

1 tablespoon lemon juice

1 cup sugar

2 tablespoons all-purpose flour

$1/2$ teaspoon cinnamon

$1/8$ teaspoon nutmeg

$1/2$ teaspoon salt

pastry for 2 (9-inch) deep-dish pie crusts

2 tablespoons butter

sugar

FRESH APPLE PIE FROM MEDINA APPLES

Pastry
(makes crust for 2 9-inch pies)

4 cups unsifted flour

1½ teaspoons salt

1¾ cups shortening

1 egg

1 tablespoon white vinegar

½ cup water

1 tablespoon vanilla

Pie filling
(for 1 pie)

10 to 12 medium Medina-grown apples, cut, peeled, cored, thinly sliced

2 tablespoons lemon juice

¾ cup brown sugar

¾ cup granulated sugar

1 teaspoon ground cinnamon

3 tablespoons flour

1 teaspoon vanilla

3 tablespoons butter or margarine

egg wash

Pastry: Combine all dry ingredients. Add shortening and cut with pastry blender to make pea-size grains. In small bowl, slightly whip whole egg, add vinegar, water, and vanilla. Pour into flour mixture and stir enough to form into 4 balls. Chill. Roll out 1 ball between 2 sheets slightly floured wax paper. Remove wax paper; place pastry in 9-inch pie pan. Roll out another ball to make top crust. Save remaining crust for a second pie.

Filling: Other apples may be used instead. Depending on size, more than 10 to 12 apples may be required for large, thick pie.

Toss sliced apples in lemon juice to coat. Add sugars and cinnamon and mix together. Put in large saucepan and cook approximately 30 minutes on medium heat (you may need to add 1 to 2 tablespoons water to make juice). During last 5 minutes of cooking, add flour and vanilla. Cool. Place in 9-inch pie pan lined with bottom crust. Pie should be filled heaping with apples. Cut butter or margarine into small pieces and place on top of apples. Cover with top crust and flute edges. Cut several slits in top crust. Using a pastry brush, gently spread egg wash on top of crust. You can, if desired, lightly sprinkle sugar and cinnamon on top.

Bake in preheated 400° oven for 10 to 15 minutes, then reduce heat to 350° and bake additional 30 to 40 minutes until "bubbly" at edges and in slits on top.

Mary Zirkel
First place winner
Medina, Texas

INTERNATIONAL GUMBO COOK-OFF 23

ORANGE

Annual. First Friday and Saturday in May

If you take a look at your Texas map, you'll find Orange is located along the Sabine River across from Louisiana. Perhaps that's one reason the folks around the area gather once a year to share legendary Texas flair and Cajun spicy foods. You'll notice the tantalizing aroma wafting its way throughout the festival grounds in downtown Orange.

Once you've had your fill of gumbo, a wide variety of food stalls provide sustenance by offering folks a choice of barbecue, shrimp-on-a-stick, sausage-on-a-stick, funnel cakes, or port-a-bobs. After all, what's a food festival for if it doesn't put a tickle in your tummy?

Much of the action begins on Friday at 5 P.M. when gumbo cook-off contestants start their roux and begin preparations for the judging activities on Saturday. You'll get a kick out of watching the chefs get their pots to boiling. Afterwards, you're welcome to kick up your heels at the jubilant dance party featuring several local bands and plenty of folks who love to strut their stuff.

Early Saturday morning folks begin lining the street in anticipation of the Gumbo Cook-off parade at 10 A.M. Once you've settled in and the parade begins, you're guaranteed a bevy of floats, bands, equestrian units, beauty-pageant winners, and dignitaries, all on tap to keep you entertained.

The remainder of Saturday has a family atmosphere. That's when everyone eats and frolics at a variety of child- and adult-oriented contests, a vendor market featuring arts and crafts, and musical entertainment.

Orange is located along Interstate 10 at the Texas and Louisiana state line. Follow the signs to downtown Orange, and you won't miss the celebration.

SPICY CAJUN GUMBO

1 pound boneless, skinless chicken, cut into strips

3 cups chicken broth

2 cups diced canned tomatoes

2 tablespoons Worcestershire sauce

1 teaspoon Cajun Seasoning Blend (recipe on next page)

1 medium onion, chopped

3 medium carrots, thinly sliced

$\frac{1}{2}$ red bell pepper, chopped

$\frac{1}{2}$ green bell pepper, chopped

1 cup sweet corn

2 teaspoons minced garlic

2 tablespoons olive oil

1 pound hot Louisiana sausage

2 tablespoons all-purpose flour

8 ounces raw shrimp, shelled, cleaned

salt and pepper to taste

hot cooked rice

filé seasoning

Place chicken, 2 cups of the broth, tomatoes, Worcestershire sauce, and Cajun Seasoning Blend in slow-cooker on high heat. In a medium skillet, sauté onion, carrots, bell peppers, corn, and garlic in olive oil for approximately 10 minutes until softened. Add to slow-cooker. In same skillet, brown sausage on all sides. Reduce heat, cover, and cook through. Slice sausages 1-inch thick and add to slow-cooker. Pour out all but 2 tablespoons of the sausage fat. Add flour and brown over medium-high heat. Stir constantly to create a very dark roux. Slowly add remaining 1 cup broth and stir until smooth. Mix roux into slow-cooker, reduce heat, cover, and cook for 6 to 8 hours. About 15 minutes before serving, stir in shrimp. Season to taste with salt and pepper. Serve over hot rice and pass the filé.

 This recipe appears along with 125 others in *Soups On!, Hot Recipes from Cool Chefs*, a cookbook I co-wrote with Gail Hobbs.

CAJUN SEASONING BLEND

Combine all spices in a small glass jar or shaker. Mix well. Store at room temperature.

$1/4$ cup salt

1 tablespoon cayenne pepper

1 teaspoon black pepper

1 teaspoon paprika

$1/2$ teaspoon chili powder

1 teaspoon granulated garlic

1 teaspoon onion powder

1 teaspoon nutmeg

1 tablespoon dried parsley

VEGETABLE GUMBO

1 teaspoon vegetable bouillon granules

¹/₂ cup white grape juice

1 onion, chopped

¹/₂ green pepper, diced

2 ribs celery, diced

1 clove garlic, minced

1 pound okra, sliced, fresh or frozen

1 pound tomatoes, fresh or canned, chopped

2 cups corn, fresh, frozen, or canned

¹/₂ cup water

¹/₄ teaspoon Tabasco sauce

¹/₄ teaspoon paprika

2 tablespoons chopped fresh parsley

1 tablespoon basil or rosemary

In a large, heavy stew pot, place bouillon, grape juice, onion, green pepper, celery, and garlic. Cook until vegetables are tender, 5 to 7 minutes. Add other ingredients. Cover and simmer until corn and okra are done. Stir occasionally to keep from sticking to bottom of pan. (Or simmer in slow-cooker for 6 to 7 hours).

Terry Poland
Oxnard, California

UNCLE BOB'S SOUP

Simmer the consommé in a saucepan. In a sauté pan add 2 tablespoons of olive oil; sauté the shrimp, scallops, and minced shallot until almost cooked. Remove from heat and set aside. Do the same with the oyster mushrooms and the asparagus. Stop just before color reaches its richest hue; broth will further cook the tender vegetables. In hot skillet add 2 tablespoons olive oil, sesame oil, and sea salt and quickly sauté the snow peas or greens; add $1/2$ cup of the hot broth to further reduce. Assemble soup by using hollow pipe (timbale) in bowl to keep greens in tubular shape. Do this in four bowls. Remove timbales from greens. Nicely arrange mushrooms, asparagus, scallops, and shrimp; top off bowls with simmering broth and fresh-ground pepper. Garnish with tarragon and serve immediately. Substitute chicken stock for the beef consommé, or use other vegetables or mushrooms. You can get creative with this soup.

Bryan's 797
Chef Bryan Lee
Beaumont, Texas

4 cups beef consommé (stock seasoned with bay, garlic, and parsley)

4 tablespoons olive oil

12 large Gulf shrimp, cleaned and peeled

12 Gulf scallops

1 shallot, finely minced

6 ounces oyster mushrooms

8 stalks asparagus, trimmed at bottom

2 tablespoons sesame oil

$1/2$ teaspoon sea salt

3 cups snow peas (dao Mei) or any tender green, cleaned and trimmed

fresh-ground pepper

tarragon seasoning to garnish

JALAPEÑO FESTIVAL
LAREDO
Annual. Third weekend in February.

24

February is the spiciest month of the year in Laredo as folks from both sides of the border join together for a *caliente* (translation: *hot*) weekend. There's top-of-the-line entertainment, appetizing food, and some fiery competitions to keep the heat on. In all, more than 2,000 volunteers work hard to raise funds for youth-oriented charities and scholarships. If you love a sizzling time and hot, fiery food, you don't want to miss this heart-warming festival.

Whether you go for the food, the competitions, the culture, the entertainment, or the crafts, you'll have a grand old time. Here are a few of the numerous events you may want to check out. Who knows, you may go home with a trophy or cash prize. Whatever you do, check 'em out.

The Jalapeño Pizza-Eating contest is open to participants thirteen to eighteen years of age. If you meet the age requirement and love a spicy pizza, this one's the right contest for you.

Adult and student chefs enter their recipes in the "Some Like It Hot!" cooking contest. The food's judged on taste and originality. The judges work up a forehead-sweat just looking at the jalapeño-filled dishes. Wait until you see what they do when they taste them.

On Saturday, the "Famous Jalapeño-Eating Contest" takes place. Participants must eat as many jalapeños as possible within a fifteen-minute time period. At the time of this writing the record is 141 devoured within the time limit. If you haven't eaten jalapeños, try one and you'll understand what a significant record this really is. You have to be twenty-one years of age to participate in this event, so bring your identification.

Trust me . . . you'll have a heck of a hot time as you experience one of the liveliest festivals held down Laredo way.

Laredo is a little bit Texas and a little bit Mexico and serves as the Texas "Gateway to Mexico." It's located on the border and along the Rio Grande River at the southern end of Interstate 35.

HOT DEVILED EGGS

1 dozen eggs, hard-boiled

1 to 2 small bottles green food coloring

6 fresh jalapeños, chopped

1 teaspoon mayonnaise

1 teaspoon hot mustard

12 olives

Cut eggs in half and set aside yolks. Brush egg whites with green food coloring. Set aside to dry. Mix yolks in bowl with jalapeños, mayonnaise, and hot mustard. Using decorating bag, squeeze mix into green eggs. Decorate with an olive on top.

Joyce Benavides
Children's entry, Jalapeño Festival
Laredo, Texas

MANICOTTI A LA MEXICANA

Boil manicotti until done and place aside. In a large skillet, cook ground beef; add salt and pepper to taste. Add tomato and spaghetti sauces, mushrooms, and jalapeño peppers. Once meat sauce is done, stuff the manicotti, place in large casserole pan, and sprinkle shredded cheese on top. Heat in 350° oven until manicotti is warm and cheese is melted.

Laura P. Garcia
First Place winner
Laredo, Texas

 Serve with a garden green salad and French bread.

16 ounces manicotti

5 pounds ground beef

salt, to taste

pepper, to taste

8 ounces canned tomato sauce

26 ounces canned spaghetti sauce

7 ounces canned mushrooms

3 jalapeños, chopped

6 ounces shredded cheese

ZESTY SQUASH CASSEROLE

8 to 10 yellow squash, cut in pieces

$1/2$ small yellow onion, chopped

$1/2$ teaspoon salt

$1/2$ teaspoon pepper

4 medium jalapeños, cooked, chopped

8 ounces packaged Velveeta cheese, cubed

8 ounces crushed tortilla chips

Boil squash until soft; drain. Pour into a casserole dish with onion, salt, pepper, jalapeños, and cheese. Bake 25 minutes at 375°. Top with crushed tortilla chips and bake an additional 10 minutes. Serve warm.

Marcy Rutherford
Laredo, Texas

MEX-TEX MENUDO COOK OFF

MIDLAND
Annual. July weekend.

25

Sponsored by the Midland Hispanic Chamber of Commerce, the annual Mex-Tex Menudo Cook Off brings out some of the finest contestants in all of Texas. It's a true West Texas weekend first celebrated over a decade ago. Tastes and textures blend to make menudo, a soup-like dish that's one of the southwest's best-known regional foods.

Menudo cooks protect their recipes from the world and from one another. What's the secret? For some it's a touch of lemon in the pot, for others it's the exact amount of onion, and still others claim success is in the fresh chili pods and oxtails. Throughout the event, spectators gather to sample the popular dish that one chef says is "a legendary cure for hangovers, lights up the tongue, livens the taste buds, and leaves off with the delicate aftertaste of oregano." Although the menudo takes center stage at the cook-off, contests also include fajitas and spicy chili dishes.

During the festival thousands of feet of shaded area are erected at Midland's Twin Cities Speedway to house the vendors who come from across town and across the Southwest. The sounds of live professional entertainment fill the air. Tejano music, evening concerts, lively dancing, and family entertainment combine to provide a venue for thousands of participants to experience an authentic celebration of heritage, art, music, dance, and cuisine.

Other attractions include games, arts-and-crafts booths, a jalapeño-eating contest, and a dunking booth. Promoted as a family-style weekend, the event offers special activities and rides for the little ones to enjoy.

Midland is situated midway between El Paso and Fort Worth along Interstate 20.

My personal experience with menudo (the soup, not the group) was limited, so I checked with Uncle Phaedrus, the talented and amazing online food guru at www.ebicom.net/ kitchen. He discovered some menudo cyber-recipes and supplied them for this section.

MENUDO SOUP

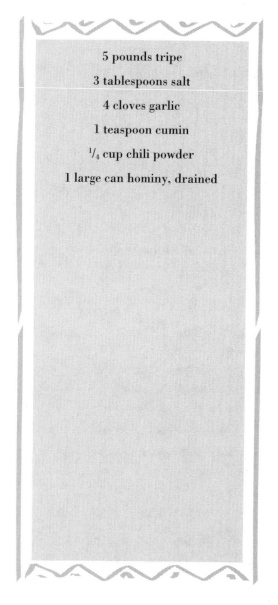

5 pounds tripe

3 tablespoons salt

4 cloves garlic

1 teaspoon cumin

$1/_4$ cup chili powder

1 large can hominy, drained

Wash tripe well and cut into 1-inch cubes. Put in a deep pot with sufficient water to cover; add salt, garlic, cumin, and chili powder. Cook until tender, about 3 hours. Thirty minutes before finished cooking, add the hominy. Adjust seasoning if necessary.

MENUDO SOUP

Put the tripe, water, onions, garlic, salt, and pepper in a large kettle. Simmer over low heat about 2 hours; skim fat off as necessary. Toast the chilies well, cut them open, and remove the seeds and veins. Grind chili skins very fine and add to the kettle. Add the cilantro leaves and simmer for another 2 hours. Add the hominy and cook for 30 minutes. Serve with the lime wedges for garnish.

6 pounds tripe, cut in 1-inch pieces

1 gallon water

2 medium onions, chopped

2 cloves garlic, mashed

1 tablespoon salt

$1/_2$ teaspoon pepper

2 ancho chilies

1 tablespoon chopped fresh cilantro leaves

7 cups cooked yellow hominy

lime wedges for garnish

MENUDO SOUP

3 pounds tripe

3 pounds hominy, frozen, thawed,
not cooked

3 pounds pigs feet, cut into quarters

1 large onion, diced

1 bunch green onions, diced

1 bunch cilantro, chopped

2 tablespoons oregano

1 tablespoon black pepper

1 tablespoon red pepper flakes

1 head garlic, peeled

2 tablespoons salt

additional fresh cilantro for garnish

additional chopped green onions for
garnish

lemon wedges for garnish

Wash tripe thoroughly, remove any excess fat, and cut into bite-sized pieces. Wash hominy and pigs feet. Combine all ingredients in a large pot with sufficient water to cover. Bring to a boil and simmer slowly until corn opens and is cooked. Skim off grease as necessary. Serve with fresh cilantro, chopped green onions, lemon wedges.

MENUDO SOUP

Cut tripe into 1-inch pieces, removing as much of the excess fat as possible. Place in a Dutch oven with veal knuckle, water, onions, garlic, salt, coriander seed, oregano, red pepper, and black pepper. Cover and simmer for 3 hours or until tripe has a clear appearance and veal is tender. Remove veal from pot; let cool, and discard bones. Chop meat and return to pot. Add undrained hominy, cover, and simmer 20 minutes. Garnish with lemon or lime wedges.

2 pounds honeycomb tripe

$1^{1}/_{2}$ pounds veal knuckle

6 cups water

$1^{1}/_{2}$ cups chopped onions

2 cloves garlic, minced

2 teaspoons salt

$^{1}/_{2}$ teaspoon coriander seed

$^{1}/_{4}$ teaspoon dried oregano

$^{1}/_{2}$ teaspoon crushed red pepper

$^{1}/_{2}$ teaspoon black pepper

15 ounces canned hominy

lemon or lime wedges

OKTOBERFEST

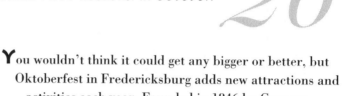

FREDERICKSBURG

Annual. First weekend in October.

26

You wouldn't think it could get any bigger or better, but Oktoberfest in Fredericksburg adds new attractions and activities each year. Founded in 1846 by German settlers, the city's charm and heritage are celebrated annually. To this day, German is still spoken throughout the community.

Festival goers discover the fun begins on colorful and popular Market Square in downtown Fredericksburg. Oktoberfest is Fredericksburg's traditional celebration of its German heritage. Every year, thousands of revelers flock to this picturesque Hill Country community to partake of food, fun, and hospitality.

Three entertainment stages mean continuous family entertainment. Over twenty-five bands perform during the three-day event. Children are entertained by a carnival with exciting rides, puppet shows and storytelling programs, sand art, and face painting. The celebration has its own on-site playground where you're apt to see a big kid or two on the swings and slides.

Fredericksburg lives up to its title of "Polka Capital of Texas" by offering continuous music and dancing. Every style of music is heard, from German to country western, along with lively waltz and polka contests and spirited sing-alongs. People come from all over to get peaches, pecans, and Opa's sausage, made in Fredericksburg.

The festival tempts modern taste buds with foods of Fredericksburg's many cultures. While most people who come to Oktoberfest claim the sausage as their favorite, other traditional food favorites include wurst, kraut, wiener schnitzel, and strudel. Also available are tempting delicacies such as fajitas, shish kabobs, turkey legs, roasted corn, and even some Cajun influence from the Caterin' Cajun. Go ahead and forget your diet. This is one time of year you should sample all that's offered.

Whether you partake of bratwurst in a beer garden, fajitas on a patio, or barbecue from a sizzling pot, you won't leave Fredericksburg feeling hungry.

Fredericksburg is located within one hour of San Antonio and Austin on U.S. Highway 290 (Austin) or Interstate 10 (San Antonio).

All recipes provided by Oktoberfest committee. They are from *Gästhaus Schmidt Kochbuch* by Donna Mittel, Fredericksburg resident.

PEACH FREEZE

2 cups chopped fresh peaches

¹/₂ cup sugar

¹/₂ cup milk

¹/₂ teaspoon vanilla

ice cubes or chopped ice

Put all ingredients in blender and fill to top with ice. Blend until smooth. Pour into cup or glass and enjoy.

Sylvia Izard
Dream Catcher Hills

OMA BLUME'S KÜSSE

(Grandmother Blum's Kisses)

Beat egg whites and sugar together, making a stiff froth. Add baking powder mixed with crumbled cracker and the pecans. Drip from spoon onto a well-greased cookie sheet. Bake about 25 minutes in a slow oven at 325°.

Mathilda Metzger Itz
Metzger's Sunday House

5 egg whites

2 cups sugar

$1/_2$ teaspoon baking powder

1 sweet cracker (saltine)

2 cups finely chopped pecans

BAKED PEACHES AND SAUSAGE

1 pound mild bulk pork sausage

1 large can peach halves

$^{1}/_{4}$ cup firmly packed brown sugar

$^{1}/_{2}$ teaspoon ground cinnamon

$^{1}/_{4}$ teaspoon ground cloves

Cook sausage until browned, stirring to crumble. Drain and set aside. Drain peach halves, reserving $^{1}/_{4}$ cup juice. Place peaches, cut side up, in a 9-inch square, well-greased glass baking dish and add reserved juice. Combine brown sugar and spices, stirring well. Sprinkle over peach halves. Bake at 450° for 15 minutes. Remove from oven and sprinkle cooked sausage evenly over top. Return to oven and bake 15 minutes.

Bob and Cathy Weidman
Acorn Street Bed and Breakfast

EASY JAMBALAYA

Crumble Jimmy Dean sausage in large pot and brown; add all vegetables, except green onions, and sauté until sausage is cooked. Add all other ingredients; stir well. Bake, covered, at 350° for 1 hour. Serve with French bread and tossed salad.

Bob and Jeanee Horner
Pedernales School House

 This recipe is easy, delicious, and requested by all who try it!

1 pound Jimmy Dean "hot" sausage

1 yellow or white onion, diced

1 bell pepper, diced

3 or 4 stalks celery, diced

1 bunch green onions, chopped

2 cloves garlic, minced

1 8-ounce can tomato sauce

$14\frac{1}{2}$ ounces canned beef bouillon

$14\frac{1}{2}$ ounces canned French onion soup

2 cups uncooked Uncle Ben's Converted Rice

$1\frac{1}{2}$ pounds sliced sausage, diced chicken, shrimp, or crawfish tails

ONION FESTIVAL
WESLACO
Annual. April date varies.

27

Here's your chance to lasso the sweet taste of Texas onions in all their glory. According to the South Texas Onion Committee, "For bigger and better sweet onions, look to the Lone Star State . . . good food is nothing to cry over!"

You'll discover plenty to keep you satisfied during this one-day event held in Harlon Block Park. Texas sweet onions are grown in the Rio Grande Valley portion of the state. The celebration attracts over 20,000 people anxious to savor the food, take in the games, shop the arts-and-crafts area, and try the full-flavored honoree. According to local organizers, the festival is an opportunity for community members, residents, and visitors to join in the fun of cooking with onions and to help promote the onion industry.

Local citizens are encouraged to participate in the Onion Recipe Contest by preparing their favorite onion dish. A panel of judges selects the winner in each of five adult and junior categories: main dish, microwave, appetizer, salad, and dessert. The annual Superb Entry Award is given at the conclusion of the recipe contest to recognize the very best sweet onion entry. It's easy to participate and you're welcome to submit your recipe prior to the contest. All you need to do to be part of the friendly warfare, action, and fun is to contact the Westlock Area Chamber of Commerce and fill out your entry form.

On the day of the event, the fun begins at 10 A.M. and the program is filled with numerous activities. Sundry arts-and-crafts merchants show and sell their wares. In addition to artwork, the area includes handmade items such as jewelry, paintings, ceramics, stained glass, and children's books.

You'll find all sorts of onion-themed souvenirs you can't live without. Countless food booths, educational and entertaining exhibits, and family activities take place throughout the day around the park's festival site. Contests include a softball tournament, basketball hoop tournament, onion-sack races, and golfing with onions. If you think par is difficult, you should try getting a birdie using an onion. Oh, how sweet it is!

An onion-clipping contest is open to onion snippers. You'll find it fascinating to watch the participants as they clip as many onions as possible during the five-minute time limit. The winner is determined by the quantity and quality of the final clipped onions. The onion-clipping contest always draws a large audience of spectators and contestants. It's exciting to watch families and friends cheer on the action.

It's said that all roads lead to Weslaco in the central Rio Grande Valley. You'll find it between McAllen and Harlingen on U.S. Highway 83.

BRAISED LAMB PROVENCAL

2¹/₂ pounds boneless lamb shoulder,
cut into 1-inch cubes

flour for dredging

2 tablespoons olive oil

2 tablespoons minced garlic

¹/₄ cup minced onion

¹/₂ cup minced red bell pepper

1 cup minced roma tomatoes

¹/₂ cup red wine

¹/₂ cup chicken stock or broth

2 tablespoons Dijon mustard

¹/₂ teaspoon thyme

¹/₂ teaspoon rosemary

¹/₂ teaspoon sage

salt and pepper to taste

Trim the lamb of fat and dredge in flour. Heat oil in pan and brown lamb well on all sides. Remove lamb, pour off all but a teaspoon of oil. Add garlic, onion, and bell pepper. Cook for 2 minutes; add the tomatoes, wine, and stock or broth. Bring to boil and reduce heat to simmer. Add reserved meat and remaining ingredients. Cover; simmer over low heat 45 minutes or until lamb is tender. Serve over hot buttered noodles or rice pilaf.

Frank Bailey, Owner
Rio Grande Grill
Weslaco, Texas

COWBOY BLUE CORN NACHOS

Spread chips in single layer on baking sheet or 12-inch pizza pan. Sprinkle evenly with onion and bell pepper, then cheese. Bake at 425°for 8 minutes or until melted and hot. If desired, top hot nachos with diced tomatoes, red chili flakes and/or spoonfuls of guacamole and sour cream.

South Texas Onion Committee
Weslaco, Texas

5 ounces blue corn or yellow corn tortilla chips

$^3/_4$ cup chopped Texas Sweet onion

$^1/_2$ cup diced sweet bell pepper

$1^1/_2$ cups grated Monterey Jack cheese

Optional for topping
diced tomatoes

red chili flakes

guacamole

sour cream

TEX-MEX CHUNKY SALSA SALAD

3 to 4 medium tomatoes, halved, seeded, cubed

1 large (14 to 16 ounces) Texas SpringSweet onion, coarsely chopped

2 cucumbers, pared, halved lengthwise, seeded, cubed

4 teaspoons minced garlic

4 jalapeños or other small, hot chili peppers, seeded, finely chopped (optional)

$1/4$ cup fresh lemon juice

1 tablespoon sugar

In medium bowl, mix all ingredients, blending well. Chill until ready to serve. If possible, make ahead so flavors have a chance to blend.

South Texas Onion Committee
Weslaco, Texas

STUFFED TEXAS SWEET ONION SHELLS

To prepare each onion for stuffing, cut a minimal slice from root end. Slice off about $^1/_2$ inch from stem end, peel, and discard skin. With small knife or apple corer, scoop out and reserve onion, using spoon as needed to make a $^1/_4$-inch-thick shell. Do not cut through bottom of shell. Each onion will hold about $^3/_4$ cup stuffing.

Chop enough scooped onion to make 1 cup and sauté with beef in oil in skillet until beef is browned. Add bean and rice mix, seasoning packet, and water called for on package. Cover, bring to boil and simmer for 20 to 25 minutes or until tender. Add corn and tomato.

Place onions in baking dish. Spoon filling into shells, mounding up. Add $^1/_2$ cup water to dish, cover and bake at 475° for 35 minutes or until onion shells are fork tender. Microwave preparation: Place stuffed onions in large, microwave-safe dish with lid, add $^1/_2$ cup water, cover and cook at full power for 20 to 25 minutes or until tender.

South Texas Onion Committee
Weslaco, Texas

4 large (14 to 16 ounces) Texas SpringSweet onions

$^1/_2$ pound lean ground beef

1 tablespoon olive or vegetable oil

4 ounces packaged seasoned black bean and rice mix

1 cup corn kernels, fresh, thawed frozen, or canned

$^1/_2$ cup chopped tomatoes

PEACH FESTIVAL

WEATHERFORD
Annual. July date varies.

There's enough going on during Parker County's Peach Festival to provide a bushel of fun and make you feel fuzzy all over. The "Peach Capital of Texas" throws a one-day party on Weatherford's historic square.

The magnificent courthouse graces the downtown area and towers regally over the event site. Scattered alongside the square's historic buildings, vendors hawk their wares, artists and craftspeople erect displays, and plenty of juicy Parker County peaches tempt the festival goers.

Folks at the chamber of commerce bill Weatherford as a "Norman Rockwell kind of town." You'll have to agree as you join the nearly 25,000 residents and visitors who assemble on the square to see the mayor do the honor of opening the festival. Miss Peach pageant winners are announced, and everyone joins in singing *The Star Spangled Banner*. This is the kind of town where neighbors greet neighbors with a hearty handshake and a tip of the cowboy hat.

At the Peach Festival there's something for everyone. Gourmands get their chance to sample tasty edibles from an assortment of booths at the Food Court, and you're apt to find the cream of the crop used in preserves, pizzas, breads, desserts, and in ways you never expected. Don't be surprised if you see plenty of folks walking through the festival site savoring a freshly picked peach as they stroll. Go ahead and try 'em all. You'll discover peach ice cream, cobblers, and even peach-based liquid refreshments.

The traditions of the Old West take place in Cowboy Country, an area that's home to old-fashioned gunfights, chuck wagon barbecues, and the rhythmic sounds of country music. Nearby, the children's amusement center beckons the little ones with tempting train rides, a petting zoo, pony rides, and enough silly clowns to entertain the entire family. Kids who want to compete may race against each other in the Diaper Derby and Toddle-Along contests.

Active adults are welcome to enter into competitions, too. If you're a biker, you may join others on the Peach Pedal Bike Ride through the serene and scenic countryside of Parker County. Or what about entering the volleyball tournaments? The popular "42" domino game was invented in the late 1800s by a Parker County resident. You'll no doubt see skilled game buffs as they eagerly test their ability to bluff the opponent.

Parker County's favorite daughter, entertainer Mary Martin, is celebrated during the festival with exhibits and displays of memorabilia depicting her movies and Broadway musical career. If you look up into the sky, you may suddenly think you see Peter Pan pass overhead.

Weatherford's peaches are found along Interstate 20 about 30 miles west of Fort Worth.

Prize-winning recipes for this section contributed by the Weatherford Chamber of Commerce.

PEACH BUTTER

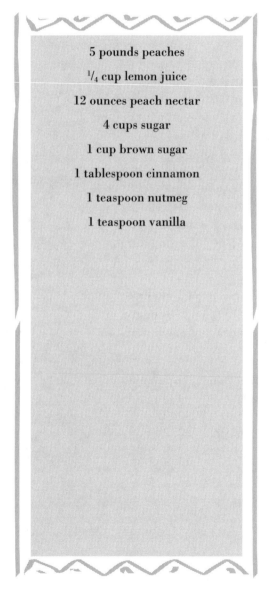

5 pounds peaches

¼ cup lemon juice

12 ounces peach nectar

4 cups sugar

1 cup brown sugar

1 tablespoon cinnamon

1 teaspoon nutmeg

1 teaspoon vanilla

Peel, pit, and purée peaches. Put peaches in a large saucepan and add lemon juice, nectar, sugars, cinnamon, nutmeg, and vanilla. Stir to dissolve sugar. Bring to a slow boil and cook, stirring often, 20 to 30 minutes or until nice and thick. Ladle into hot sterilized jars, clean rims, and seal. Process in a hot-water bath for 10 minutes. Fills 10 half-pint jars.

Brenda Slate
First Place winner
Arlington, Texas

TEXAS PEACH AND BLUEBERRY PIE

Line pie pan with bottom crust. Combine all ingredients and gently toss. Spoon mixture into pie crust. Add top crust, seal and brush ever so lightly with milk, and sprinkle with sugar. Bake at 400° for 45 minutes.

Sally Brumbaugh
Second Place winner
Weatherford, Texas

pie crust for 2 9-inch pies

Pie filling

$^3/_4$ cup sugar

$^1/_2$ cup packed brown sugar

$^1/_2$ cup flour

$^1/_2$ teaspoon cinnamon

$^1/_4$ teaspoon allspice

3 pints fresh blueberries

1 cup fresh chopped peaches

1 tablespoon lime juice

1 tablespoon melted butter

milk and sugar for topping

GRANDMA BEARD'S PEACH COBBLER

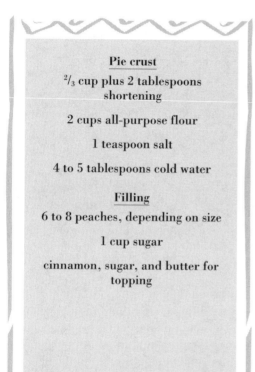

Pie crust

²/₃ cup plus 2 tablespoons shortening

2 cups all-purpose flour

1 teaspoon salt

4 to 5 tablespoons cold water

Filling

6 to 8 peaches, depending on size

1 cup sugar

cinnamon, sugar, and butter for topping

Pie crust: Cut shortening into flour and salt until particles are size of small peas. Sprinkle with water, 1 tablespoon at a time, tossing until all flour is moistened. May add 1 to 2 teaspoons more water if necessary. Divide into 2 balls. Roll out each ball until ¼-inch thick and set aside.

Filling: Peel, pit, and slice peaches. Put a layer of peaches into a 9 x 13-inch pan. Sprinkle ½ cup sugar over peaches. Cut one rolled-out pie dough into strips and crisscross over peaches. Add second layer of peaches and sprinkle with ½ cup sugar. Cut the remaining rolled-out crust into strips and crisscross over peaches. Sprinkle top layer of dough with cinnamon and sugar; dot generously with butter. Bake at 375° until top is brown, about 45 minutes.

Kathy Higginbottom
Weatherford, Texas

PEACH JAMBOREE & RODEO

STONEWALL

Annual. Third weekend in June.

29

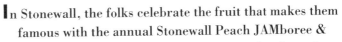

In Stonewall, the folks celebrate the fruit that makes them famous with the annual Stonewall Peach JAMboree & Rodeo. The events are more than peachy, featuring a rodeo, parade, washer pitching, peach show, and some arts and crafts. Peach Patch is where kids find face painting, games, a petting zoo, and more than enough excitement to keep them on the go.

The festivities begin on Friday at 6:30 A.M. with a kickoff breakfast at the Stonewall Fire Station. Peach pie and cobbler entries are due by 10 A.M. at the Stonewall Chamber of Commerce on Saturday, and the JAMboree parade begins at 10 A.M. on St. Francis Street and Ranch Road.

The donated proceeds help defray the cost of beautifying the community. You don't want to stay eating too long, though. The deadline for the preserve contest is Friday at 8:30 A.M. and you won't want to miss your chance to enter your favorite recipe.

The rodeo begins Friday at 8 P.M. That's when the hootin' and hollerin' rock the arena with special activities including a kids' calf scramble, clown specialty acts, and the glittering introduction of the Peach Queen candidates. The rodeo features bareback riding, calf roping, team roping, bull riding, and jackpot barrel racing for the ladies. After all that, you're likely to barely have enough energy to do some stompin' and kickin' at the big dance beginning at 9:30 P.M.

Saturday the fun kicks off during the 10 A.M. parade and the simultaneous baking contest at the fire station. At 11 A.M., the barbecue-by-the-pound begins and the food and beverage booths open. Get your plate filled early because the fiddlers contest begins at noon and you don't want to miss it.

The afternoon brings with it a peach show and judging along with the Gillespie County Peach Queen Pageant. Then it's time for the auction of prize-winning peaches, preserves, and baked goods, musical entertainment, and another night of rodeo action. Get there on time. The drums roll promptly at 8 P.M. as the coronation of the Peach Queen takes place during the opening of the rodeo. It might not be Miss America, but it's darn close, and you'll want to be there to watch the royalty crowned.

If your energy holds out, there's another dance after Saturday's rodeo and then home to bed. Remember to get up early the next day and leave plenty of time to savor some of those delicious peach preserves and peach cobbler you brought home with you.

Stonewall, The Peach Center of Texas, is located about 60 miles west of Austin on U.S. Highway 290.

PEACH PRESERVES

Place peaches into 2-quart stainless cookware. Add lemon juice, margarine, and fruit pectin. Bring mixture to rolling boil (one that cannot be stirred down). Add sugar and bring mixture to rolling boil for one minute and remove from heat. Place into hot sterilized jars. Makes approximately 7 half-pint jars.

Bob Hopper
Stonewall, Texas

This recipe seems to work best if 3 cups of ripe and 2 cups firm peaches are used.

5 cups peeled, sliced peaches

2 tablespoons lemon juice

$\frac{1}{2}$ teaspoon margarine

1 box fruit pectin

6 cups sugar

FRESH PEACH PIE

Filling
3 cups peeled, sliced, fresh peaches

1½ cups sugar

2 tablespoons cornstarch

1 teaspoon vanilla

1 tablespoon butter

pie crust for 2 9-inch pies, unbaked
(recipe below)

butter and sugar for topping

Crust
1 cup butter

2 cups flour

½ cup brown sugar

½ teaspoon salt

ice water

Filling: Mix all ingredients together and bring to a boil. Put in pie shell. Cover with another crust, crimp, and cut a few slits in upper crust. Brush with melted butter and sprinkle with sugar. Bake at 325° for 45 minutes or until crust is golden brown.

Crust: Mix all ingredients together; add enough ice water until dough stays together. Roll into 2 equal parts for top and bottom of pie.

Lisa Schmidt
First Place
Stonewall, Texas

PEACH COBBLER

Mix crust ingredients; roll out half of crust and put into a 8 x 8-inch pan. Pour in peaches. Roll out other half of crust; cut into strips. Place strips over peaches. Sprinkle sugar and cinnamon over strips. Bake at 350° until golden brown.

Jerome Jenschke
First Place
Stonewall, Texas

Crust
3 cups flour

1 teaspoon salt

1 cup yellow Crisco

1 egg plus water to make $\frac{1}{2}$ cup

Filling
$2\frac{1}{2}$ cups peeled, sliced peaches, sweetened with sugar to taste

sugar and cinnamon for topping

WHITWORTH'S PEACH ICE CREAM

5 to 6 eggs

2 cups sugar

1 quart half-and-half

1 pint heavy whipping cream

1 can condensed milk

5 to 6 peaches, peeled and cut into tiny pieces

Beat eggs and sugar together. Mix in remaining ingredients except peaches. Pour into ice cream maker and process according to manufacturer's instructions. Add peaches while processing.

Daryl Whitworth
Fredericksburg, Texas

 Let sit in ice cream maker, covered with a towel, for about $^1/_2$ hour after finishing the processing. Doing this adds to the flavor and consistency.

NELDA VOGEL'S PEACH BUTTER

Purée unpeeled peaches in a food processor. Mix all ingredients together in a large saucepan or kettle. Bring to a hard boil, stirring constantly. Continue stirring and boiling for 10 to 15 minutes. Remove from heat. At this point the butter can be covered and refrigerated.

Nelda Vogel
Fredericksburg, Texas

 Use the peach butter within a week or so. For longer use, the butter may be canned by using traditional canning methods.

16 cups unpeeled peaches

8 cups sugar

2 teaspoons cinnamon

1 teaspoon nutmeg

PECAN FESTIVAL

GROVES

Annual. Last full weekend in September.

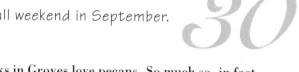

Folks in Groves love pecans. So much so, in fact, their annual celebration has been declared the official Texas Pecan Festival by the Texas House of Representatives. According to one local newspaper writer, the good people of Groves enjoy the tiny, tawny Texas pecan so much they "grow 'em, throw 'em, bake 'em, eat 'em, and celebrate 'em."

The Pecan Festival is far and away the town's biggest visitor attraction of the year, with an attendance of nearly 50,000 pecan lovers and aficionados. What brings so many people to the family-style event is a long and varied list of activities. The weekend gets underway with the popular Pecan Festival Parade. Crowds of people fill the downtown streets to watch clowns, bands, floats, and the Groves Pecan Queen. Although many people come for the pecan-based menu, competitive sports enthusiasts aren't left out. Sporting events held throughout the weekend include tennis, archery, softball, and volleyball tournaments, and a 5K run.

Speaking of food, old and young alike love the pie-eating and cooking contests. Depending on who's cooking, you're apt to find the likes of Southern pecan pie, bread pudding, pecan chicken, pecan crescents, and even a Texas-style pecan pizza.

Country and Cajun music bring their rhythm to Lions Park on Friday and Saturday nights with dance and choral groups, along with young local vocalists and twirlers rounding out the tasteful entertainment menu. Other activities include the Texas Pecan Festival Queen's Pageant, antique show, art show, and a chance to enter your favorite pet in the Pecan Festival Pet Show.

Groves is located north of Port Arthur and south of Orange on Texas Highway 87.

All recipes for this section provided by the Groves Chamber of Commerce & Tourist Center.

PECAN PIZZA

Preheat oven to 350°. Beat butter, sugar, and vanilla until fluffy. Stir in combined oats and flour. Divide dough into 4 equal portions. Place 2 portions on opposite corners of a large ungreased cookie sheet; press each into a circle about $1/8$-inch thick, and press $1/2$-inch of the outer edges with tines of a fork. Repeat with other 2 portions. Bake 15 to 20 minutes or until lightly brown. Remove from oven and spread preserves on center of each circle; sprinkle with chopped pecans. Cool 10 minutes on cookie sheet, then cut each circle into 8 wedges; cool completely and serve.

1 cup margarine or butter, softened

$1/2$ cup sugar

1 teaspoon vanilla

2 cups oats, quick or old fashioned, uncooked

$1^1/_4$ cups flour

$1/2$ cup fruit preserves, mix red and yellow

chopped pecans

THE ONE AND ONLY PECAN PIE

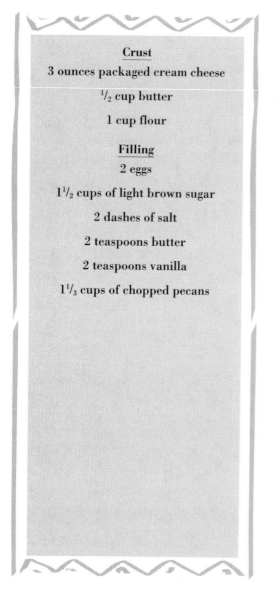

Crust

3 ounces packaged cream cheese

½ cup butter

1 cup flour

Filling

2 eggs

1½ cups of light brown sugar

2 dashes of salt

2 teaspoons butter

2 teaspoons vanilla

1⅓ cups of chopped pecans

Crust: Mix ingredients together, chill, and shape the dough to fit your pie pan.

Filling: Beat all ingredients together, except the pecans, until smooth. Then fold in pecans. Pour the filling into the pie crust. Bake at 350° for 50 minutes or until done. Cool before serving.

PECAN CHICKEN

Place each piece of chicken between two sheets of wax paper; flatten to $1/4$-inch thickness using a meat mallet or rolling pin and set aside. Combine honey and mustard; spread on both sides of chicken, then dredge chicken in chopped pecans. Arrange chicken in a lightly greased, shallow baking pan. Bake at 350° for 30 minutes or until chicken is tender.

4 chicken breast halves, skinned and boned

$1/4$ cup honey

$1/4$ cup Dijon mustard

$1 1/2$ cups finely chopped pecans

NIBBLERS

2 cups all-purpose flour

1 teaspoon ground red pepper

$^{1}/_{2}$ teaspoon salt

1 cup butter, softened

2 cups (8 ounces) shredded sharp
cheddar cheese

1 cup finely chopped pecans

2 teaspoons dill seed or dill weed

Preheat oven to 350°. Combine flour, ground pepper, and salt; set aside. In a medium bowl, cream butter and cheese. Stir in flour mixture, then the nuts and dill. Roll teaspoons of dough into balls. Place on ungreased cookie sheet and bake 15 to 18 minutes or until golden brown. Makes about 55 balls.

NUTTY BUTTERY PECAN CRESCENTS

Sugar syrup: Boil water and sugar together in a saucepan over medium heat for 20 to 30 minutes or until slightly thickened.

Crescents: Mix flour, $1/4$ cup sugar, baking powder, and salt together. Combine hot butter with warm water and slowly add to flour mixture until it looks like biscuit dough (soft). Roll out thin and cut in round circles like biscuits. Mix pecans and remaining $1/4$ cup of sugar together. Place heaping teaspoon of pecan and sugar mixture on top of dough. Bring sides together to make crescent shape; close edges by pinching with fingers or with a fork. It should look like a half-moon or crescent. Place on cookie sheet and bake at 350° for 20 to 25 minutes or until light brown. When crescents come out of oven and are still warm, dip them in sugar syrup.

Sugar Syrup
(Prepare before starting crescents.)

2 cups water

2 cups sugar

Crescents

6 cups flour

$1/2$ cup sugar, split

1 teaspoon baking powder

$1/2$ teaspoon salt

1 cup hot melted butter

$3/4$ cup warm water

3 cups finely chopped pecans

PRAIRIE DOG CHILI COOK OFF & WORLD CHAMPIONSHIP OF PICKLED QUAIL EGG EATING

GRAND PRAIRIE

Annual. First weekend in April.

31

Who could resist a celebration with a name like this one? This Texas-sized salute to chili, the official state dish, serves up some mighty fine chili (not necessarily made out of prairie dog meat), prepared by some of the best barbecuers in all of Texas. During the event, there's plenty planned to keep the whole family active for an entire jovial weekend.

Held at Traders Village in Grand Prairie, this colorful event is the granddaddy of all North Texas-area chili cook-offs. You'll be among 75,000 people having one heck of a time kicking up their heels and downin' some right fine vittles. What's more, the event is free (but the parking is two bucks a vehicle).

Chili cooks from as far away as the state of Tennessee are joined by Texas chiliheads (as they affectionately call themselves) on Saturday. As many as forty cooks, ages eight to eighteen, hone their budding culinary skills in the Junior Division. At the same time, the adults warm up for Sunday's chili competition by participating in the "Ranch-Style Beans—Winner Takes All—Pinto Bean Blowout."

You'll surely want to join in Saturday's schedule of free contests. There's the Invitational Eat-and-Run Stewed Prune Pit-Spitting Contest, the Original Anvil Toss, the Chicken-Flying Contest, and the Lemon Roll.

During the World Championship of Pickled Quail Egg-Eating contest, contestants see how many of the hard-boiled gourmet delights they can consume in sixty seconds.

Enter and who knows, you may be the one to walk away with the traditional, coveted, hand-painted commode-seat trophy.

While chili cooking is the main purpose of this two-day celebration, having fun is the underlying reason for participating. Zany chili and team names, inventive costumes, elaborate cooksite setups, and audience involvement by teams all ensure your good time and an unforgettable festival finale.

Traders Village is located at 2602 Mayfield Road in Grand Prairie, off Texas Highway 360. Website location: www.tradersvillage.com

BEEF CHILI

Chili

2 teaspoons vegetable oil

1 pound lean beef cubed steaks

Spicy Seasoning Mix, recipe follows

1 medium onion, chopped

salt to taste

28 ounces canned plum tomatoes, undrained

2 cups frozen whole kernel corn, thawed

Spicy Seasoning Mix

3 tablespoons chili powder

2 teaspoons ground cumin

$1^1/_2$ teaspoons garlic powder

$^3/_4$ teaspoon dried oregano leaves

$^1/_2$ teaspoon ground red pepper

Chili: Heat oil in deep, large skillet over medium heat 5 minutes. Cut each beef steak lengthwise into 1-inch-wide strips, then cut crosswise in 1-inch pieces. Sprinkle beef with 2 teaspoons Spicy Seasoning. Stir-fry beef and onion 2 or 3 minutes. Season with salt, if desired, add tomatoes (break up with back of spoon), corn, and additional $2^1/_2$ teaspoons Spicy Seasoning. Bring to a boil, reduce heat to medium-low and simmer, uncovered, 18 to 20 minutes.

Spicy Seasoning Mix: Combine all ingredients. Store, covered, in airtight container. Shake before using.

Texas Beef Council
Austin, Texas

 Serve with tortilla chips and melon wedges.

SPICY PORK CHILI

In a 4-quart Dutch oven, cook pork, onion, green pepper, and garlic in hot oil until pork is browned. Stir in flour, mixing well. Add the remaining ingredients, except cheese and tortillas. Simmer, uncovered, for one hour. Top each serving with some of the cheese. Serve with tortillas, if desired.

National Pork Producers Council
Des Moines, Iowa

$1^1/_2$ pounds boneless pork loin, cut into 1-inch pieces

1 medium onion, coarsely chopped

1 medium green pepper, coarsely chopped

1 clove garlic, minced

1 tablespoon vegetable oil

1 tablespoon all-purpose flour

32 ounces canned whole peeled tomatoes, crushed

32 ounces canned red kidney beans

8 ounces canned tomato sauce

3 tablespoons chili powder

1 tablespoon ground cumin

1 teaspoon salt

$^1/_2$ teaspoon black pepper

$1^1/_2$ cups shredded cheddar cheese (6 ounces)

warm flour tortillas, optional

THAI CHILI CHICKEN

oil for sauté pan

4 ounces canned chopped green chilies

3 cloves fresh garlic, chopped

8 ounces chicken breast, cut into cubes

1 medium onion, sliced

1/2 pound mushrooms, sliced

juice of 1/2 lime

2 teaspoons brown sugar

2 teaspoons oyster sauce, optional

2 teaspoons low-salt soy sauce

4 bunches fresh cilantro

Heat oil in wok or deep, heavy pan over high heat. Add chilies and garlic; fry until crisp and golden, about 2 minutes. Drain chilies and garlic onto paper towels, but leave oil in the wok or pan. Fry chicken and onion in remaining oil until chicken is cooked, about 3 to 4 minutes. Add mushrooms, lime juice, and sugar and fry about 2 minutes. Add sauces and mix thoroughly for 1 minute. Remove to serving plates and sprinkle with cilantro.

Ray Finfer, Creator
Death by Chili
Irving, Texas

 Serve over rice or noodles, or alone.

CHUCKWAGON CHILI

In large skillet, brown the beef cubes and garlic in hot oil; drain off excess fat. Add beef broth, water, oregano, sugar, cumin seed, salt, and bay leaves. Reduce heat and simmer, covered, until the meat is tender, about 1½ hours. Stir in the chilies and cornmeal. Simmer 30 minutes, covered, stirring occasionally. Remove bay leaves before serving.

John Thorton
Grand Prairie, Texas

 Serve with cornbread and a green salad.

2½ pounds beef round steak, cubed

1 clove garlic, minced

3 tablespoons cooking oil

10½ ounces canned beef broth

1½ cups water

2 teaspoons crushed dried oregano

1 teaspoon sugar

1 teaspoons crushed cumin seed

½ teaspoon salt

2 bay leaves

4 ounces canned chopped green chilies

2 teaspoons cornmeal

RED STEAGALL COWBOY GATHERING & WESTERN SWING FESTIVAL

FORT WORTH

Annual. October weekend.

32

If it has anything to do with cowboys or the cowboy way of life, you'll find it at the Red Steagall Cowboy Gathering & Western Swing Festival. The event promotes western heritage and the cowboy lifestyle. The weekend event takes place at the Stockyards National Historic District in Fort Worth.

Red Steagall, noted singer and entertainer, is the founder of the event that bares his name. Steagall is also a top cowboy poet and was named the "Official Cowboy Poet of Texas" in 1991.

Two special features of the gathering are the children's poetry contest and the Western Swing Fest. The kids' contest is divided into two age groups and participants are asked to write poems about ranching or cowboy life. All finalists recite their work during the event. In the tradition of Milton Brown, Harry Choates, and Bob Wills & His Western Playboys, western swing music enthusiasts tap their toes, sway to the rhythm, and almost dance their boots off during the Western Swing Fest. Cowboy musicians, horn players, guitar pickers, and Dixieland aficionados join forces to play and dance during this popular activity of the gathering.

Additionally, the Cowtown Trading Post and Cowboy Exchange brings more than 100 vendors from throughout the Southwest to sell quality cowboy gear and western merchandise. The majority of the merchandise is handmade with workmanship of the highest quality. Music has always been a major part of the western lifestyle, and it plays a major part in the celebration. Featuring some of the best swing music in the state, plenty of professional musical groups will get you and your partner dancin' the night away.

Other major events include the authentic chuck wagon competition sanctioned by the Western Chuck Wagon Association. You don't want to miss the grand parade as it officially opens the event. Teams of horses and mules pull the chuck wagons from downtown Fort Worth into the Stockyards at high noon on Friday. It's a great opportunity to see how chuck wagons played an important part on cattle drives. In keeping with tradition, the cooks exhibit their skills by preparing beef, beans, bread, and desserts in an authentic camp setting. If you're lucky, you may be able to talk some of them into sharing a recipe or two.

Truly a family affair, this extraordinary event includes all the hustle and bustle of the activities listed above plus horsemanship clinics, a cowboy-trappings show, and a ranch horse and team sale. It's the place to be if you're a big or little cowpoke or simply a wannabe.

The Stockyards National Historic District, home of the Red Steagall Cowboy Gathering, is located at 130 East Exchange Avenue in Fort Worth.

TIN PLATE SPECIAL

1 pound pinto beans

5 pounds rump roast

1 tablespoon lard or shortening

1 cup banana-pepper or green-pepper strips

2 medium onions, sliced

2 cups tomato juice

8 ounces canned tomato sauce

$^{1}/_{2}$ cup water

2 tablespoons cider vinegar

2 tablespoons brown sugar

2 tablespoons salt

1 tablespoon dry mustard

1 tablespoon thyme

Wash beans, cover with cold water, and let soak overnight. Bring beans to boil and cook 1 hour; drain. Brown roast in hot fat in large Dutch oven, add peppers and onions, and cook until almost tender. Add beans and remaining ingredients. Cover and bake at 350° for 2$^{1}/_{2}$ to 3 hours, or until beans are tender.

Billy J. Huckaby
Cowtown Coliseum
Fort Worth, Texas

FEIJOADA

Cover the beans with water and soak overnight, or cover them with boiling water and let stand two hours; drain. Preheat oven to 350°. In a large Dutch oven, combine beans with the 6 cups of water and remaining ingredients. Bring to a boil, skimming if necessary. Cover and transfer to oven. Bake 1 1/2 hours, remove cover, and bake another 30 minutes, stirring occasionally. Serve with cornbread, if desired. Or allow to cool slightly, then cover and refrigerate overnight. Remove any fat from surface and reheat slowly.

National Pork Producers Council
Des Moines, Iowa

1 pound dried black beans

sufficient water to cover beans

6 cups water

1 pound boneless ham, cut into
3/4-inch pieces

1 pound boneless pork loin, cut
into 3/4-inch pieces

3/4 pound hot Italian sausage,
sliced into 1-inch pieces

3/4 pound smoked sausage, sliced
into 1-inch pieces

1 pint cherry tomatoes, stemmed

1 onion, peeled, chopped

1 teaspoon red pepper flakes

6 cloves garlic, peeled, minced

1/8 teaspoon orange zest

BARBECUED BEEF AND BEAN SOUP

2 pounds beef sirloin tip roast, cut into ¹/₂-inch cubes

3 cups chopped onion

3 garlic cloves, minced

2 tablespoons vegetable oil

2 tablespoons chili powder

2 tablespoons ground cumin

¹/₄ teaspoon ground cloves

1 teaspoon salt

¹/₂ teaspoon pepper

64 ounces canned tomatoes with juice, chopped

48 ounces canned pink or pinto beans, drained

14 ounces bottled, roasted red bell peppers, drained, rinsed, chopped

3¹/₂ cups beef broth

¹/₄ cup molasses

1 tablespoon Tabasco

2 teaspoons cider vinegar

Brown beef, onion, and garlic in oil in large Dutch oven over medium heat. Stir in chili powder, cumin, cloves, salt, and pepper. Add tomatoes, beans, peppers, broth, molasses, and Tabasco. Simmer over low heat for 1¹/₂ hours, partially covered, stirring occasionally. Stir in vinegar and serve.

Texas Beef Council
Austin, Texas

 Great served with sourdough bread and vegetable relishes.

TEXAS POTATOES

Mix first 5 ingredients and 1 cup of shredded cheese. Put in greased 13 x 9 x 2-inch casserole dish. Top with remaining cheese and corn flake crumbs; drizzle with remaining margarine. Bake, uncovered, at 400° for 45 to 50 minutes.

Patty Fessenden
Mission, Texas

1 large package or 2-pound bag frozen hash browns, thawed, drained

$\frac{1}{2}$ cup chopped onion

$\frac{1}{2}$ cup melted margarine, divided (save $\frac{1}{4}$ cup for topping)

2 cans cream of chicken soup, undiluted

8 ounces sour cream

2 cups shredded cheddar cheese, divided

1 cup corn flake crumbs

RENAISSANCE FESTIVAL

PLANTERSVILLE

Annual. October–November.

The gates of the Texas Renaissance Festival open like the pages of a fairy tale full of gallant knights and lovely ladies recreating the romance of the Renaissance era. Strolling through the shaded glens of the sixteenth-century New Market Village, lords and ladies marvel at the multitude of jugglers, jesters, magicians, and minstrels. You're invited to escape to the revelry and romance where drama and grandeur unfold all around you.

Fun and frolic enfold the kingdom as brave knights, with lances drawn, joust for their honor and the hands of the fairest maidens in the land. Chivalry prevails over chariot races as drivers charge full-speed around the royal Tournament Field. Only the strongest of mind and body reign during seven weekends of music, mayhem, and merriment.

Noblemen and peasants alike enjoy the competitive spirit of the archery and axe-throwing contests, fencing matches, and King of the Log competition. Go ahead and Drench-a-Wench or make your way through The Amazing Maze; you'll feel you're living in days of yore. The children of the kingdom are invited to make merry on the King's Carousel, ride the Flying Dragons, climb Jacob's Ladder, and dance around the Maypole.

Authentic demonstrations of ancient artistry capture the excitement of Elizabethan times as potters, glass blowers, blacksmiths, broom makers, and wood coopers display their talents and sell their wares.

The Texas Renaissance Festival takes place in a permanent fifty-acre theme park with a picturesque pine forest. The European Renaissance comes to life with nearly fifty unique rides and games, along with music and comedy on eleven main stages, a magnificent marketplace of more than 250 arts-and-crafts shops, exquisite food and drink from around the world, and grandly costumed characters filling the grounds.

Plantersville is located about 50 miles northwest of Houston on Old San Antonio Road (Texas Highway 105). Website location: www.texrenfest.com

All recipes for this section are from my book, *Food Festivals of Southern California* (Falcon Publishing Company, Inc.).

GOLDEN APPLES OF MEAT

4 to 6 small red potatoes

butter

a dash of thyme

1 onion, finely chopped

1 mushroom, finely chopped

1 carrot, finely chopped

1 pound ground sirloin

2 tablespoons Worcestershire sauce

salt and pepper to taste

pie crust dough

1 egg

red food coloring (optional)

Bake potatoes in ovenproof dish with butter and thyme for about 15 minutes or until tender. Set aside and allow to cool. Sauté onion, mushroom, and carrot in butter for one minute. Add to ground sirloin. Add Worcestershire sauce and salt and pepper to taste. Wrap meat mixture around the potatoes to form meatballs with potatoes in center. Fry meatballs in skillet until brown. Wrap each meatball in pie crust dough and mold into apple shape. Brush with beaten egg and bake at 375° for about 20 minutes. When removed from oven, brush with a small amount of red food coloring, if desired.

Louise Jurgens
Renaissance Pleasure Faire
San Bernardino, California

EGGS IN FRENCH ROLLS

Cut the rolls in half and scoop out some of the center bread. Toast the inside of the roll and spread with butter. Break an egg into each half roll and season with salt and pepper. Bake at 350° approximately 20 to 30 minutes or until the eggs are set. Sprinkle the orange juice over the eggs and serve very hot.

Renaissance Pleasure Faire
San Bernardino, California

 Legend has it this hot feasting dish was prepared in the early 1700s.

4 French rolls

butter for spreading

8 eggs

salt and pepper

juice from 1 or 2 oranges

SCULPTURED HONEY WHOLE WHEAT BREAD

2 envelopes yeast

$^1/_2$ cup warm water

$^1/_2$ cup honey

$1^1/_2$ cups milk

4 ounces clotted cream or cream cheese

3 cups whole-wheat flour

$^1/_2$ cup wheat germ

$1^1/_2$ teaspoons salt

$2^1/_4$ to $2^1/_2$ cups all-purpose flour

1 tablespoon water

Sprinkle yeast over warm water in a 2-cup measuring cup. Add 1 teaspoon of the honey; stir to dissolve and let stand 10 minutes. In medium-sized saucepan. Heat milk and clotted cream or cream cheese until well blended; cool to lukewarm. Stir in yeast mixture. Stir in whole-wheat flour, wheat germ, and salt until smooth. Stir in enough flour to make a soft dough. Knead till smooth and elastic (10 minutes). Place in large buttered bowl and cover with a damp towel. Let rise about 1 hour or until doubled in bulk. Punch down and turn onto floured surface. Knead a few times and cover with bowl to rest 10 minutes. Butter pan; shape dough to desired sculpture. Cover with towel and let rise in warm place 45 minutes. Combine water and remaining honey and brush on bread. Bake in preheated oven at 325° for 45 minutes.

Lisa Lennaco
Renaissance Pleasure Faire
San Bernardino, California

RICE FESTIVAL
WINNIE
Annual. Beginning the last weekend in September.

34

The Texas Rice Festival celebrates everything to do with rice and good times. Since 1969 the festival has been a week-long, annual event. It's a tribute to generations of rice farmers and the Texas agriculture industry. The event provides a country fair atmosphere popular with families who enjoy being together.

Each year as the rice bows to the harvesting machines, locals and tourists crowd the Winnie-Stowell Park to view a million-dollar farm equipment display, rice-threshing demonstrations, a rice-cooking contest, and rice education exhibits.

More than 100,000 people attend the festival annually, kicking off the event with the BBQ and Fajita Cookoff, Open Horse Show, and Go Texan Activities. The festival offers a wide variety of entertainment and activities from gospel music to carnival rides. Street dances are held and food offerings include rice balls, gumbo, étouffée, pistolettes, blooming onions, crab, pork-ka-bobs, and more. The event is renowned for its cuisine.

Friday is set aside as a day dedicated to young people. Activities and schedules are planned especially for them. Youth Day includes a 4-H and Future Farmers of America Livestock Show, Junior Queen contest, Miss Laterite contest, Little Rice King contest, Diaper Derby, Scavenger Hunt, Face Painting, and the Youth Day Parade. Saturday hosts the Grand Parade with dozens of floats, bands, farm equipment, royalty, and dignitaries. It's followed by live entertainment on the main stage. Throughout the weekend, lively programs incorporate a Rice-Eating Contest, craft shows, and an evening street dance. Exhibits feature quilts, photography, and art.

The friendly folks of Winnie are found about 25 miles southwest of Beaumont along Interstate 10.

RICE-BREAD PUDDING

1   30-inch loaf fresh French
bread

1½ cups cooked rice

3 eggs, slightly beaten

2 cups whole milk

2 cups heavy cream or
evaporated milk

2 cups granulated sugar

2 tablespoons vanilla extract

½ cup raisins

¼ cup butter

Break up bread into small pieces. Put into a large mixing bowl. Add cooked rice. In another bowl mix eggs, milk, heavy cream or evaporated milk, sugar, and vanilla extract. Pour mixture over bread and rice. Mix with your hands, squeezing bread and pushing down into milk mixture until bread and rice are saturated. Allow to stand for 10 minutes.

Boil raisins for 3 to 4 minutes and leave in water until cool. Drain raisins and add to bread mixture. Meanwhile melt butter and pour into a pan large enough for the entire mixture to fill halfway. Preheat oven to 350°. Pour mixture into buttered pan and even out from end to end and side to side. Bake for 45 minutes or until completely brown on top. (Note: if ends are browning too fast and middle is not cooking as fast, lower the temperature and extend the cooking time until top is cooking as fast. Then lower temperature and extend cooking time until top is browned).

Ann Mattingly
First Place, Women's Division
Hamshire, Texas

ZUCCHINI, SQUASH, AND WILD RICE CASSEROLE

Preheat oven to 350°. Grease a large baking dish. Layer all ingredients and seasonings, reserving 1 cup of cheese and sliced tomatoes for the top. Bake, covered, about 45 minutes. Remove cover and place tomato slices on top of casserole. Sprinkle top with remaining cheese. Return to oven until cheese is melted. Serve hot. Makes 10 to 12 servings.

Margaret (Peggy) Jones
Grand Champion, Senior Citizen Division
Stowell, Texas

2 zucchini squash, sliced

4 yellow squash, sliced

1 medium onion, diced

8 ounces canned or fresh sliced mushrooms

10 ounces packaged frozen chopped spinach, cooked and drained

2 cups cooked wild or plain rice

1 teaspoon oregano

1 teaspoon basil

salt and pepper to taste

3 cups shredded mozzarella cheese

1 or 2 tomatoes, sliced

CAJUN RICE AND SAUSAGE BRAID

$^1/_2$ cup corn oil margarine, divided

12 ounces packaged light regular turkey-and-pork sausage

1 medium onion, chopped

$^1/_2$ green or red bell pepper, chopped

3 stalks celery, chopped

3 tablespoons dried parsley

10$^1/_2$ ounces canned tomatoes with chilies

10$^1/_2$ ounces canned cream of mushroom soup

1 teaspoon black pepper

$^1/_2$ teaspoon garlic powder

1 cup uncooked rice

16 ounces canned crescent dinner rolls (2 8-ounce cans)

1 egg

Melt 2 tablespoons margarine in medium-size Dutch oven, add sausage, and cook until no pink remains. Spoon off any grease. Remove sausage and set aside. Melt remaining margarine in Dutch oven and sauté onion, bell pepper, and celery until tender. Return sausage to Dutch oven along with parsley, tomatoes, soup, black pepper, and garlic powder. Add rice and cover. Bake in preheated 375° oven for about 45 minutes to 1 hour, until rice is done. Set aside to cool.

Open both cans of crescent rolls and remove dough. Lay one rectangle of dough from first can on top of rectangle from second can. With rolling pin, roll dough into 16 x 10-inch rectangle. Place on ungreased cookie sheet. Spoon lukewarm sausage-rice mixture down the center of the rectangle. Make 2$^1/_2$ cuts at 1-inch intervals on both sides of rectangle. Overlap strips of dough alternating all the way down the loaf. Brush with egg wash. Bake at 375° until light brown or about 15 to 20 minutes.

Beverly K. Tudor
Reserve Grand Champion
Main Dish Women's Division
Port Neches, Texas

To create eggwash, beat the egg with a tablespoon of water.

SASSAFRAS FESTIVAL
SAN AUGUSTINE COUNTY
Annual. October weekend.

35

The goal of the Sassafras Festival is to promote the historical values of San Augustine County. It's held in the city of San Augustine, home of the largest sassafras tree in the state. A native tree of East Texas, it displays brilliant-colored foliage in the fall. It also offers three exotic aromas from its roots, wood, and leaves. The roots smell of root beer, the wood smells like medicines, and the leaves smell of citrus. You certainly want to take the guided tour during the festival to see the much-heralded San Augustine tree. Special transportation and knowledgeable guides make the journey past historic locations to the site of the privately owned champion tree.

Round up the loved ones. During the weekend, there's plenty for every member of the family to do, see, and taste. For the serious barbecue cooker, the BBQ Cookoff, sanctioned by the East Texas BBQ Cookers Association, offers a competition that produces award-winning recipes and opportunities to advance to regional and statewide barbecue recognition.

A bit more laid back, but competitive just the same, the Gumbo Cookoff produces some of the best gumbo in all of Texas. All the gumbo made and served must include, as a side dish, filé, a thickening agent made from powdered sassafras leaves. Cooks have a choice of using it in the gumbo as well but it's not required. Barbecue and gumbo chefs are required to use a piece of sassafras wood in the cooking of their entries. If you adore gumbo, you'll want to pick up a copy of the chamber of commerce's *Gumbo Cookbook*.

Once you've had your fill of gumbo and barbecue, along with sassafras tea, jelly, and candy, you'll no doubt want to take a stroll around the San Augustine County courthouse and visit the arts-and-crafts vendors with their handmade wares. Nearby, you'll discover the magnificent collection of eye-popping vintage cars on display. These cars are owned by county residents who take great pride in showing off their highly polished and prized treasures. Also on display are antique tractors and farm equipment used to till the East Texas soil.

Schedule time to enjoy the lively Sassafras Festival Pet Parade. You'll get a kick out of the kids and their pets all dressed up in their best parade finery. It's fun, frivolous, and guaranteed to put a smile on your face. You and your pet are welcome to join in the parade, so if you have one, bring it along.

San Augustine County is called "The Cradle of Texas." It's a place where Sam Houston walked, Davy Crockett was feted on his way to the Alamo, and J. Pinckney Henderson, Texas's first governor, lived. The city of San Augustine lies near the Louisiana border on Texas Highway 21.

CHICKEN AND SAUSAGE GUMBO

Boil chicken until tender to make broth; remove skin and bones from broth. A good roux is a must! Use iron skillet and wooden spoon. Heat oil until very hot; add flour. There should be enough to "take up" all oil. Stir roux constantly over medium heat until it's a deep brown. This process cannot be rushed and may take as long as 20 minutes. Remove from heat. Pour into a large pot with chicken and broth. Add the rest of the ingredients, except for sausage, green onions, parsley, and filé. Cook until vegetables are tender. Add sausage, green onions, and parsley. Cook about 3 to 5 minutes, add filé, and serve over rice.

Gumbo Cookbook
Mary Leach Rushing
DeRidder, Louisiana

1 stewing chicken

$^1/_2$ cup oil

$1^1/_2$ cups flour

1 cup chopped celery

1 large onion, chopped

salt and pepper to taste

3 cloves garlic, chopped

3 bay leaves, crushed

1 teaspoon basil

1 teaspoon thyme

$^1/_8$ teaspoon cayenne pepper

$^1/_8$ teaspoon chili powder

$^1/_2$ pound link sausage, cooked, sliced

2 bunches green onions, chopped

$^1/_2$ cup parsley, chopped

2 teaspoons gumbo filé or to taste

TURKEY GUMBO

remains of a turkey, cleaned and cut

salt and pepper to taste

cayenne and Tabasco to taste

$\frac{1}{2}$ pound lean ham, cut in small pieces

1 large onion, finely chopped

3 pieces of parsley, finely chopped

1 sprig of thyme, finely chopped

4 tablespoons butter

2 quarts water

$\frac{1}{2}$ red pepper, finely chopped

1 bay leaf

3 dozen fresh oysters with stock

2 tablespoons filé

Clean and cut turkey and add salt, pepper, cayenne, and Tabasco to taste. Cut ham into small pieces, and add onion, parsley, and thyme. Put the butter into soup kettle; add ham and turkey when hot. Fry for 10 minutes. When brown, add stock from oysters and 2 quarts of water. Add red pepper and bay leaf. Simmer for 1 hour. Bring to a boil, add fresh oysters, cook for about 5 minutes, and remove from heat. Have tureens ready. Only then add filé. It can only be heated once. Serve over rice. Never boil the gumbo with rice and never add filé while the gumbo is on the fire.

Gumbo Cookbook
Curt Goetz
San Augustine, Texas

Have you ever wondered how to use the leftovers from a holiday turkey? After boiling the carcass, remove remaining turkey meat, dice it into $\frac{1}{2}$-inch pieces, and use it to create this hearty turkey gumbo.

SEAFOOD GUMBO

Make a roux by browning flour in well-heated vegetable oil. Lower heat and add water gradually. Add onion, garlic, bell pepper, and parsley. Simmer 30 minutes. Add crab meat. Crab may be freshly cleaned, fresh, or frozen lump crab meat, but it is nice to have the crab claws and a few chunks from the body of the crab in the gumbo. Add bay leaves, Worcestershire sauce, and seasonings, but save the filé. Cook about 15 minutes. Add shrimp and oysters and cook about 5 minutes on high heat until oysters begin to curl. Do not overcook shrimp and oysters. Turn heat off, add filé, and serve. Filé is powdered sassafras leaves and is a thickener, so don't overdo it. A tablespoon is about right. If you cannot find filé, add thinly sliced, young, tender okra at the beginning for thickening.

Gumbo Cookbook
Ernest Easley
San Augustine, Texas

$^1/_2$ cup flour

$^1/_2$ cup vegetable oil

2 quarts or more of water

1 large onion, chopped

1 clove garlic, chopped

$^1/_2$ bell pepper, chopped

$^1/_4$ cup chopped parsley

1 pound crab meat

2 bay leaves

1 tablespoon Worcestershire sauce

salt and pepper to taste

Tabasco sauce to taste

2 pounds shrimp

1 quart oysters with oyster water

filé to taste

4 to 5 okra

ORIENTAL SHORT RIB BARBECUE

4 pounds beef rib short ribs,
trimmed and cut crosswise, no
more than $^3/_8$ to $^1/_2$-inch thick*

$^2/_3$ cup thinly sliced green onions

$^1/_2$ cup soy sauce

$^1/_2$ cup water

$^1/_4$ cup dark sesame oil

$2^1/_2$ tablespoons packed brown
sugar

$1^1/_2$ tablespoons crushed toasted
sesame seeds

1 tablespoon minced garlic

1 tablespoon grated fresh ginger

$^1/_2$ teaspoon ground red pepper

$^1/_8$ teaspoon freshly ground
Szechuan peppercorns**

fresh red chili peppers for
garnish

green onions for garnish

radish roses for garnish

Combine sliced green onions, soy sauce, water, sesame oil, brown sugar, sesame seeds, garlic, ginger, red pepper, and Szechuan peppercorns; reserve $^1/_2$ cup marinade. Place beef ribs and marinade in plastic bag, turning to coat. Close bag securely and marinate in refrigerator 4 to 6 hours, turning occasionally. Remove ribs from marinade, place ribs on grill over medium coals,*** and grill 5 to 6 minutes. Turn ribs over and brush with reserved marinade. Cover and continue cooking 5 to 6 minutes or until desired doneness is reached. Place ribs on platter; garnish with chili pepper, green onion, and radish roses.

*Beef rib short ribs, cut $^3/_8$- to $^1/_2$-inch thick may be special ordered from your meat retailer. Each rib piece should contain 3 cross-cut rib bones.

**Szechuan peppercorns are available in the Oriental section of the supermarket. Freshly ground black pepper may be substituted for the Szechuan peppercorns.

***Test about 4 inches above coals for medium with 4-second hand count.

Texas Beef Council
Austin, Texas

SCARBOROUGH FAIRE, THE RENAISSANCE FESTIVAL

WAXAHACHIE

Annual. Late April through June.

36

Have you ever attended a Renaissance-themed event? If not, here's a delightful way to begin. If so, then you certainly don't want to miss the annual Scarborough Faire.

For those not in the know, a Renaissance Festival celebrates the music, mirth, and merriment of sixteenth-century Europe. The Scarborough Faire is one of the largest and most popular events in Texas and comes complete with entertainment, crafts, food, drink, games, and plenty of robust fun. Hundreds of prominent entertainers perform, more than 200 artisans display and demonstrate their crafts, and food and beverage vendors offer a delicious variety of over sixty menu items fit for a king, queen, noble, or peasant.

With ten stages offering continuous entertainment and two full combat jousts a day, you'll discover music and laughter rings throughout the village of Scarborough in Waxahachie. During your visit to the festival, you'll savor the atmosphere of sixteenth-century costumes, customs, and careers being celebrated by hundreds of characters greeting you in the streets of the village. You can listen to madrigal groups, watch living chess matches, observe the Royal Parade and knighting ceremonies, and cheer the performers during maypole dances and dramatic sword play challenges.

Scarborough Faire hosts hundreds of world-class artisans from across the country. The crafts are unique, handmade (some right before your eyes), and ready to be whisked away. In addition you can view glassblowers, a Gutenberg press, the Crown Jewels, and a hall of armor with its authentic weaponry, shields, and armor.

If you love food, the Faire's the place to be. The more-than-sixty menu items include enormous turkey legs, Grecian gyros, chicken on a stake, sausage on a skewer, and much more. Five major food areas are spread throughout the 35-acre village. You'll be tempted by a wide variety of foods and flavors, from refreshing fruit concoctions to hearty entrees to satisfying sweets.

Bring the family and enjoy knighting reenactments performed by King Henry VIII and Queen Anne Boleyn, turtle races, face painting, the petting zoo, fortune telling, palm reading, hair braiding, and a school preparing you for knighthood.

The Faire is located on an expansive 35-acre wooded site near Waxahachie, 30 minutes south of Dallas and Fort Worth, off Interstate 35E south at exit 399A. From Austin or Waco, follow Interstate 35E north to exit 399.

All recipes for this section provided by Scarborough Faire, the Renaissance Festival.

YE ROYAL SCOTCH EGGS

Mix flour and chili; coat each hard-boiled egg with the mixture. Then coat each egg with the ground ham. Mix ground bread, bread crumbs, sage, and salt. Dip the ham-coated eggs into the beaten eggs and roll in the bread crumb mixture. Fry in approximately 3 inches of oil at 360°for 5 to 6 minutes or until a deep golden brown in color. Serve warm if possible, with a spicy mustard.

$1^1/_2$ cups all-purpose flour

6 teaspoons chili powder

48 hard-boiled eggs, shelled

6 pounds sugar-cured ground ham

$4^1/_2$ cups wheat bread, ground

3 teaspoons white bread crumbs

$1^1/_2$ teaspoons ground sage or to taste

$1^1/_2$ teaspoons salt

24 eggs, well beaten

RED BEANS AND RICE

4 pounds dried red beans

6 quarts cold water

4 cups chopped yellow onions

2 bunches green onions, chopped

$\frac{1}{8}$ cup granulated garlic

2 bunches parsley, chopped

6 pounds sausage, cut into chunks

Wash and pick through beans. Put beans in a large pot and add enough cold water to cover. Add onions and garlic; bring to a boil. Cover and cook at a slight boil for 1 hour. Add the remaining ingredients and more water, if necessary; cover and simmer for 2 hours or until beans are soft. Remove 2 cups of the cooked beans without juice and mash. Return them to pot and stir; this thickens the soup. If necessary, add water to thin the beans.

 Serve over rice with a corn bread muffin on the side.

ÉTOUFFÉE

Sauté bell peppers, yellow onions, green onions, and celery in butter. When tender, add red pepper, salt, black pepper, and soup. Simmer for 20 to 25 minutes. Turn off the fire, add shrimp, put on lid, and let cook until shrimp turns pink. Mix the cornstarch with the water until smooth. Thicken the recipe by slowly adding cornstarch solution until desired consistency is reached.

 Serve over rice in a bread bowl.

$4\frac{1}{2}$ bell peppers, chopped

$4\frac{1}{2}$ yellow onions, chopped

$4\frac{1}{2}$ bunches green onions, chopped

6 stalks celery, chopped

3 cubes butter

red pepper to taste

salt to taste

black pepper to taste

75 ounces canned cream of mushroom soup

9 pounds shrimp, thoroughly rinsed and drained

4 tablespoons cornstarch

$1\frac{1}{2}$ cups water

SHRIMPOREE

ARANSAS PASS

Annual. Third weekend in September.

37

Every year the population in Aransas Pass increases by more than 60,000. For a weekend, anyway. That's because once a year the Shrimporee fills Aransas Pass Community Park with shrimp and the people who love to eat them.

The Shrimporee festival, a celebration of the shrimp industry, has grown in both attendance and attractions for more than fifty years. As the name suggests, almost any kind of shrimp is available and prepared in almost every imaginable way at the weekend event.

Culinary concoctions involving the crustacean include Cajun-style shrimp, shrimp creole, fried shrimp, boiled shrimp, shrimp gumbo, shrimp kabobs, jambalaya, and shrimp egg rolls. Some shrimp even do time on the "bar-be." Other dining options are available too.

Participants wishing to show just how full their fill is may enter a shrimp-eating contest. It's an event which held the *1976 Guinness Book of World Records* title. Entrants have thirty minutes to chew, swallow, gulp, or otherwise ingest all the shrimp they can hold.

Food's not the only reason for you to attend this shrimp-oriented function, however. The Great Outhouse Race travels down Commercial Street and reflects a tongue-in-cheek takeoff on Montezuma's Revenge. Participants build and drag their "house of the crescent moon" down the main street of town and the trotter who pulls a privy across the finish line first wins the prizes.

Those who find pulling their potties too hot a job often opt to enter the Cool Meltdown competition. Entrants use body heat to turn a solid block of ice into a lukewarm puddle of water. According to organizers, "No body part is disallowed, although accepted societal norms of decency are in effect." The meltdown event is the Aransas Pass answer to "there's going to be a hot time in the old town."

Once you've eaten all you want, about 150 arts-and-crafts vendors offer something for everyone. Booths include wooden fish and shrimp items, shell articles, clothing, crafts, gifts, curiosities, art, antiques, and jewelry. As you'd expect, many of the items for sale include a sea-life theme.

Along with hot food, cool deals, and cold beverages, you can pick up your own official Shrimporee of Texas postage stamp cancellations and participate in events such as a bicycle rodeo, early morning 5K run and 2K walk, the Shrimporee parade, a carnival complete with many popular rides, and various other family-oriented attractions.

The Aransas Pass Shrimporee takes place on the official Shrimporee grounds at Aransas Pass Community Park just south of downtown on Texas Highway 361. Website location: info@aransaspass.org

All recipes in this section developed by Annette Reddell Hegen, Seafood Consumer Education Specialist.

SHRIMP CONFETTI

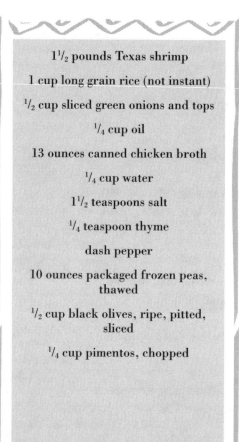

1½ pounds Texas shrimp

1 cup long grain rice (not instant)

½ cup sliced green onions and tops

¼ cup oil

13 ounces canned chicken broth

¼ cup water

1½ teaspoons salt

¼ teaspoon thyme

dash pepper

10 ounces packaged frozen peas, thawed

½ cup black olives, ripe, pitted, sliced

¼ cup pimentos, chopped

Peel and de-vein shrimp. In large skillet, heat rice and green onions in oil. Add chicken broth, water, salt, thyme, and pepper. Mix well. Bring to boil, cover and simmer 15 minutes, or until rice is nearly done. Add shrimp and remaining ingredients. Cover and cook over low heat for 5 minutes or until shrimp is done.

OVEN-FRIED CURRIED SHRIMP

Peel shrimp, remove veins, and wash. Combine egg and water. In separate container, combine crumbs, curry powder, salt, and pepper. Dip shrimp in egg and roll in crumbs. Place on a well-greased baking sheet. Drizzle oil over shrimp. Bake at 500° for 10 minutes or until golden brown. Serve with Hot Marmalade Soy Dip.

2 pounds Texas shrimp

1 beaten egg

1 tablespoon water

1 cup toasted bread crumbs

2 teaspoons curry powder

$1/2$ teaspoon salt

dash pepper

$1/4$ cup cooking oil

Hot Marmalade Soy Dip
(recipe on next page)

HOT MARMALADE SOY DIP

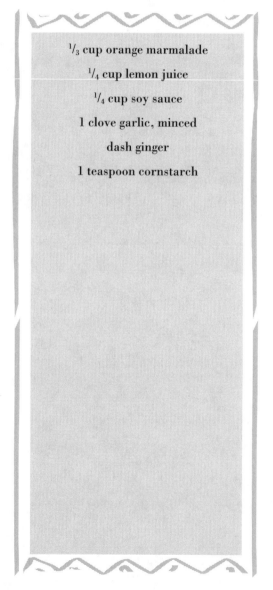

1/3 cup orange marmalade

1/4 cup lemon juice

1/4 cup soy sauce

1 clove garlic, minced

dash ginger

1 teaspoon cornstarch

Combine ingredients and mix well. Cook over low to medium heat, stirring constantly, until clear and thickened. Serve hot with shrimp. This makes about 3/4 cup of dip.

BROILED SHRIMP CHEESIES

Chop shrimp and mix with mayonnaise, cheese, and onion. Spread mixture on bread slices; place slices on baking sheet. Sprinkle with paprika. Broil 4 inches from heat source until hot and bubbly. Serve immediately. Makes about 20 hors d'oeuvres.

$^1/_2$ pound cooked Texas shrimp

1 cup mayonnaise

1 cup grated Parmesan cheese

$^1/_4$ cup minced onion

party or cocktail rye bread

paprika

TEXAS SEA SLAW

3 cups chopped red cabbage

3 cups chopped green cabbage

$^1/_2$ cup grated carrots

$^1/_3$ cup snipped fresh parsley

$^1/_3$ pound cooked, chopped shrimp

$^1/_3$ pound cooked, flaked fish

1 cup light mayonnaise

1 cup buttermilk

1 package original Hidden Valley
Ranch dressing mix

In a large mixing bowl, combine red and green cabbage, carrots, and parsley. Fold in seafood. To prepare dressing, mix remaining ingredients in a small container. Add to salad and mix thoroughly. Serve cold as a main dish or side dish with assorted crackers.

SPINACH FESTIVAL
CRYSTAL CITY
Annual. Second weekend in November.

38

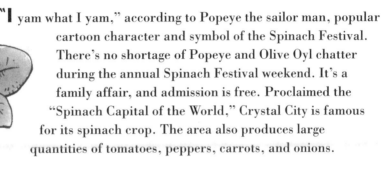

"**I** yam what I yam," according to Popeye the sailor man, popular cartoon character and symbol of the Spinach Festival. There's no shortage of Popeye and Olive Oyl chatter during the annual Spinach Festival weekend. It's a family affair, and admission is free. Proclaimed the "Spinach Capital of the World," Crystal City is famous for its spinach crop. The area also produces large quantities of tomatoes, peppers, carrots, and onions.

Whether you're a comic character buff, festival fanatic, or gallivanting gourmand, you're bound to get a muscle workout during a weekend of diversion and merriment. Want to really become part of the action? You're invited to wear Popeye or Olive Oyl attire if you wish.

The festivities get under way with the annual Spinach Kickoff Dance held at the Crystal City Ballroom prior to the main festival. The elaborate pageant and crowning of the Festival Queen and her court are designed to get you in the mood for the events that follow.

The parade, with its 120 or so entries, is always delightful and entertaining. It gets underway on Saturday when crowds begin claiming parking spaces and site locations prior to the kickoff. Always one of the highlights of the festival, the procession attracts visitors from around the United States. Naturally, there are plenty of comic characters scattered among the cheerleaders, vintage cars and trucks, bands and their boosters, family entries, floats, schools, marching units, and the event's very own Popeye.

The Spinach Cook-off is held Sunday. People young and old from all parts of the country compete for awards and trophies. Categories are vegetable dishes, salads, main entrees, dips, and hors d'oeuvres. It doesn't matter your age, everyone is invited to flex their muscles and enter a favorite spinach dish. Age categories include adult, pre-teen, juniors, and seniors.

Throughout the weekend, popular musicians, music legends, and Music Hall of Fame honorees entertain. In addition, spectators have an opportunity to extend a hand to performing Ballet Folkloric groups from around the region.

Nearly 60,000 visitors join the 8,000 residents of Crystal City and are invited to participate in all the activities. There's a softball tournament, the annual Spinach Festival Golf Tournament, several fitness runs and walks, and a car show that attracts participants from all over the country.

What makes the Spinach Festival unique and successful? It's the warm and friendly hospitality of the residents of Crystal City. You'll find them 120 miles southwest of San Antonio on U.S. Highway 83.

SPINACH NUGGETS

In a saucepan, combine spinach and dried onion. Cook according to package directions. Drain well. In mixing bowl, combine spinach mixture, croutons, and cheese. Stir in eggs and melted margarine. Shape into 1-inch balls. Place in shallow pan. Cover and freeze. At serving time, place frozen nuggets in shallow baking dish. Bake at 375° for 15 to 20 minutes or until thoroughly heated.

Maria Alcorta
Crystal City, Texas

20 ounces packaged frozen chopped spinach

1 tablespoon minced dried onion

2 cups herb-seasoned stuffing croutons

1 cup grated Parmesan cheese

2 eggs, beaten

3 tablespoons margarine, melted

SPINACH BALLS

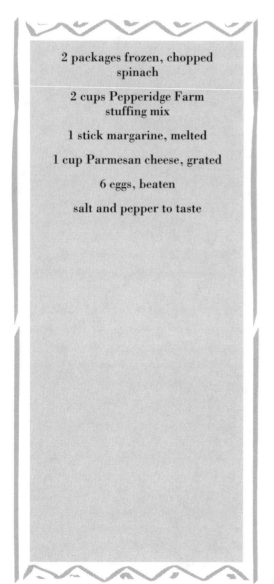

2 packages frozen, chopped spinach

2 cups Pepperidge Farm stuffing mix

1 stick margarine, melted

1 cup Parmesan cheese, grated

6 eggs, beaten

salt and pepper to taste

Cook spinach as directed on package; cool before handling. Lightly squeeze all water out of the spinach. Mix all ingredients and form balls about the size of ping-pong balls. Bake at 350° for 15 minutes.

Virginia Payne
Crystal City, Texas

After baking, these spinach balls may be frozen for future use.

SPINACH SQUARES

Preheat oven to 350°. Combine milk, butter, onion, parsley flakes, Worcestershire sauce, salt, thyme, and nutmeg. Add beaten eggs and mix well. Add spinach and rice and pour into greased casserole. Cook 15 minutes. Top with cheese and return to oven for 5 to 10 minutes. Cut into squares.

Emalee Carruthers
Crystal City, Texas

$1/_3$ cup milk

2 tablespoons butter

$1/_2$ cup minced onion

1 tablespoon dry parsley flakes

$1/_2$ teaspoon Worcestershire sauce

$3/_4$ teaspoon salt

$1/_2$ teaspoon thyme

$1/_2$ teaspoon nutmeg

2 eggs, beaten

10 ounces packaged frozen spinach, cooked, drained

1 cup cooked rice

10 ounces packaged shredded American cheese

SPINACH DIP

2 jars chopped baby food spinach

$^1/_2$ teaspoon minced parsley

$^1/_2$ teaspoon salt

1 teaspoon pepper

1 cup instant minced onion

2 cups mayonnaise dressing

few drops lemon juice

Mix all ingredients; let stand 5 to 6 hours in refrigerator.

Korena Orozco
Crystal City, Texas

STRAWBERRY FESTIVAL

POTEET
Annual. First weekend in April.

Some people think life's a bowl of cherries. Well, in my book, it's also a bowl of apples, peaches, watermelon, and strawberries.

The annual Poteet Strawberry Festival is one of the largest and most popular festivals in Texas. The population of the small town of Poteet swells to upward of 200,000 viewers of the Saturday Parade and trek through the festival grounds. In all, they spend a berry bright summer weekend surrounded by plenty of premier Texas strawberries.

You'll be inspired to taste a variety of strawberry foodstuffs. Along with the famous and totally delicious Poteet strawberry shortcake, vendors offer strawberry bread, strawberry cheesecake, chocolate-dipped strawberries, strawberry fudge, and special Texas strawberry ice cream. For wine lovers, the Poteet Strawberry Festival Association dispenses tasty wines and coolers.

Throughout the weekend, ten areas of continuous entertainment are provided by professional performers including nationally known country and western artists, Texas gunfighters, hypnotists, ventriloquists, thrill shows, ethnic dancers, and regional bands. There's always plenty of special entertainment, including a carnival for youngsters and teens. Other weekend attractions include an arts-and-crafts show, two performances of the Festival Rodeo, and a "Taste of Texas" food show and auction.

The ninety-five acre Poteet Strawberry Festival site is located on Texas Highway 16 just 25 miles south of San Antonio. There's free parking and complete RV facilities. Website location: www.strawberryfestival.com

STRAWBERRY FIESTA BREAD

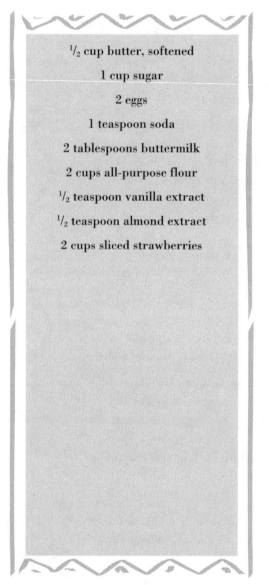

¹/₂ cup butter, softened

1 cup sugar

2 eggs

1 teaspoon soda

2 tablespoons buttermilk

2 cups all-purpose flour

¹/₂ teaspoon vanilla extract

¹/₂ teaspoon almond extract

2 cups sliced strawberries

Cream butter, gradually adding sugar. Beat until light and fluffy. Add eggs, one at a time, beating well after each addition. Dissolve soda in buttermilk, add to batter, and mix well. Stir in flour. Add vanilla and almond extracts and stir well. Gently stir in strawberries. Spoon into 2 greased 7¹/₂ x 3 x 2-inch loaf pans. Bake at 350° for about 45 minutes. Turn out on wire rack to cool.

Poteet Strawberry Festival Committee
Poteet, Texas

STRAWBERRY PIZZA

Crust: Combine flour and sugar; cut in butter. Pat mixture into pizza pan. Bake 15 minutes at 325°. Cool. Beat together remaining ingredients until fluffy. Spread over cooled pastry.

Topping: Combine thawed strawberries, sugar, and cornstarch. Cook over medium heat until thickened. Cool. Spread on top of cream cheese pastry. Arrange fresh strawberries as final topping. Cover with plastic wrap. Refrigerate at least 2 hours. Cut into pizza-like wedges.

Becky Duncan
Grand Champion
Poteet, Texas

Crust

1 cup flour

$^1/_2$ cup powdered sugar

$^1/_2$ cup butter

8 ounces packaged cream cheese

$^1/_2$ teaspoon vanilla

$^1/_2$ cup sugar

$^1/_4$ teaspoon lemon juice

Topping

10 ounces packaged frozen strawberries, thawed

4 tablespoons sugar

1 tablespoon cornstarch

1 pint fresh strawberries, sliced

FRENCH STRAWBERRY PIE

1 quart fresh strawberries

1 6-ounce package cream cheese, softened

1 9-inch baked pie shell

1 cup sugar

3 tablespoons cornstarch

whipped cream

Wash and drain strawberries. Spread softened cream cheese (with a little sugar added) over baked pie shell. Cover cream cheese with half of the choicest berries, standing them upright. Mash remaining berries until juice is extracted. If necessary, add a little water to make $1\frac{1}{2}$ cups of juice. Bring juice to a boil and gradually stir in sugar and cornstarch. Stir constantly over moderate heat until mixture thickens and boils. Boil 1 or 2 minutes. Cool and pour over berries in pie shell. Chill 2 hours. Remove from refrigerator 20 minutes before serving. Add whipped cream.

Poteet Strawberry Festival Committee
Poteet, Texas

STRAWBERRY BUTTER

Wash, hull, and slice berries. Sprinkle with sugar and let stand for 30 minutes to 1 hour. Drain, reserving juice. Cream butter or margarine in a blender or processor and gradually add powdered sugar. After all is fluffy, blend in vanilla and strawberries. Chill before serving. Don't throw away the strawberry juice, add it to a fresh fruit salad.

Poteet Strawberry Festival Committee
Poteet, Texas

 Serve with hot biscuits or bread.

$1\frac{1}{2}$ cups strawberries

4 tablespoons sugar

1 stick butter or margarine

2 cups powdered sugar

1 teaspoon vanilla

ELEGANT STRAWBERRY ROMANOFF PIE

4 ounces packaged vanilla pudding and pie filling mix

3 ounces packaged strawberry gelatin

2 cups water

3 tablespoons orange liqueur or orange juice

8 ounces frozen whipped topping, thawed

1 pint strawberries, hulled

1 baked 9-inch pie shell, cooled

Combine pudding mix, gelatin, and water in saucepan. Cook and stir over medium heat until it comes to a boil. Add liqueur or juice and chill until thickened. Beat in 2 cups of the whipped topping. Arrange whole strawberries with pointed ends up in pie shell, reserving several for garnish. Top with filling and chill 2 hours. Garnish with remaining whipped topping and reserved strawberries.

Ruth Carson
Poteet Strawberry Festival Committee
Poteet, Texas

TOMATO FEST

JACKSONVILLE
Annual. Second Saturday in June.

The small city of Jacksonville celebrates the tomato in style when everyone gets together and puts on the annual Tomato Fest. Held in downtown Jacksonville, the most fun of all comes during a wide variety of contests and competitions, all tomato-themed. Although the tomato isn't as important to the Jacksonville economy as it once was, this day-long event keeps the town's tomato tradition alive.

It takes forty cases of tomatoes to keep the teams going during the Battle of San Tomato. Held at the Tomato Bowl, the battle pits two teams of twenty-five people against one another in the tomato fight of their lives.

Home-grown Cherokee County tomatoes are judged during the Best Home-Grown Tomato Contest. No store-bought imitations are allowed. If you've been cultivating your prized tomato all season long, now is the time to pick it and bring it with you for judging of its color, shape, and taste.

Contestants in the Tomato-Eating Contest have three minutes to devour all the tomatoes they can. There's no charge to participate in the cooking event, but recipes must be submitted with each of the entries. Enter any tomato dish you want. It's fine to bring some of Granny's canned stewed tomatoes or your favorite salsa dip.

Tomato Tales are scheduled throughout the event, and local historians describe Jacksonville as it was during the booming tomato years. Other activities keeping the most ardent tomato fancier happy include the Couch Tomato No Sweat Olympics, a variety of entertainment, arts-and-crafts booths, hot-sauce contest, farmer's market, and the Tomato Shoot.

Jacksonville lies due south of Tyler, Texas, along U.S. Highway 69.

PICANTE SAUCE

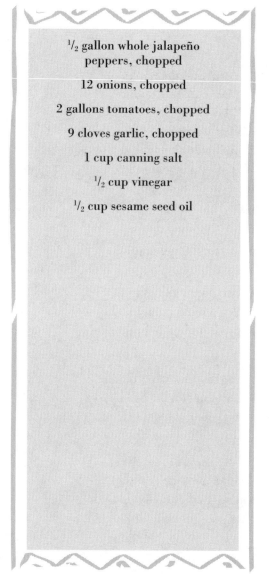

½ gallon whole jalapeño peppers, chopped

12 onions, chopped

2 gallons tomatoes, chopped

9 cloves garlic, chopped

1 cup canning salt

½ cup vinegar

½ cup sesame seed oil

Put all ingredients in large pot; stir well. Bring to a boil that cannot be stirred off. Place in sterile jars until sealed. Makes 20 pints.

Evette Morris
Jacksonville, Texas

Medium Hot Salsa

Core and chop peeled tomatoes. Combine with all other ingredients in large saucepan. Bring to boil, stirring frequently. Reduce heat and simmer about 45 minutes. Fill 8 hot pint jars. Remove trapped air bubbles. Cap and hot water bath about 20 minutes.

Steve Mims
Jacksonville, Texas

5 pounds ripe tomatoes, peeled
(approximately 8 cups)

3 cups chopped onions

1 cup cider vinegar (5% acidity)

1 cup seeded and chopped
jalapeño peppers

3 teaspoons salt

TOMATO CONSOMMÉ

4 cups canned whole tomatoes

4 cups V-8 vegetable juice

4 cups tomato juice

4 cups chicken stock

$^1/_4$ cup garlic pearls

$^1/_4$ cup chopped fresh basil

5 skinless chicken breasts, ground

10 egg whites

diced tomatoes for garnish

In a 2-gallon stockpot, combine tomatoes, V-8 juice, tomato juice, chicken stock, garlic, and basil. Simmer for $1^1/_2$ hours and remove from heat. Pass tomato stock through a medium-grade strainer (do not blend), then pour the tomato stock back into the stockpot; side aside. Whip ground chicken and egg whites with an electric mixer on slow speed until they are well combined. Stir into tomato stock. Bring to a boil, reduce to a low heat, and simmer for 45 minutes. Pass mixture through cheese cloth. Garnish with diced tomatoes and serve hot.

The French Room, The Adolphus
Dallas, Texas

COWBOY CATSUP

In large pot, cook tomatoes, peppers, and onions together without adding water. Strain and measure pulp (4 quarts); add salt, sugar, and spices. Place whole spices in a gauze bag during cooking and remove before pouring catsup into jars. Ground spices, except paprika, will darken catsup. Cook ingredients, except vinegar, rapidly for 1 hour. Add vinegar and cook until thick.

Recipes from Across the United States
Family Travel Log
Kewanee, Illinois

$1/2$ peck tomatoes, chopped
(about 4 quarts)

3 red peppers, chopped

2 medium onions, chopped

2 tablespoons salt

2 teaspoons celery salt

$1/3$ cup sugar

2 teaspoons ground mustard

1 tablespoon whole allspice

1 tablespoon whole cloves

1 tablespoon cinnamon

1 teaspoon paprika

2 cups vinegar

TOMATO-BASIL PASTA WITH GARLIC-BASIL CHICKEN

1 tablespoon butter

2 boneless, skinless chicken breasts

2 teaspoons crushed garlic

2 teaspoons basil

8 cups water

2 tablespoons olive oil, divided

1 16-ounce package Garden Rotini Pasta

1 tablespoon balsamic vinegar

1 teaspoon basil

4 tablespoons minced garlic

3 Roma tomatoes, diced

Parmesan cheese, grated, for topping

Melt butter and brush over chicken on both sides. Sprinkle with garlic and basil. Bake in 450° oven for 20 to 25 minutes, or until done, or cook on grill until done. Dice chicken into bite-sized pieces.

In large saucepan, bring water and 1 tablespoon olive oil to a boil. Stir in pasta; boil until tender. Drain. Stir in rest of olive oil, vinegar, basil, garlic, tomatoes, and chicken. Serve hot, topped with Parmesan cheese. Add more basil and garlic to suit taste.

Pam Anderson
Jacksonville, Texas

UNCLE FLETCH'S HAMBURGER COOK-OFF & AMERICAN MUSIC FESTIVAL

HENDERSON COUNTY

Annual. Fourth Saturday in May.

Folks come from far and near to enjoy the Battle of the Bands, Hamburger Cook-off, and the Great Bowls of Fire Chili Cook-off at Henderson County's Uncle Fletch's Hamburger Cook-off & American Music Festival held in Athens, Texas. Wonder why? Here's the answer: Athens is recognized as the home of the hamburger! There's a historical marker at the Henderson County courthouse square that reads: "On this site in the late 1880s, cafe owner Fletcher Davis . . . made the first hamburger sandwich." Encouraged by Athens' enthusiasts, he introduced the sandwich at the 1904 St. Louis World's Fair. What could be more fitting than an annual celebration of the hamburger and all that it stands for?

Celebrate much of what makes America and Texas famous at this festival held in downtown Athens. The day begins at 9 A.M. when the hamburger and chili teams set up for a day of competition. Always different, burger chefs vie for the "world's best burger" title with entries that include the likes of Athens' Piñata Burger, Lizard Burger, Spicy Cactus Burger, and the Uncle Fletch All-American Hamburger Burger. With names like that, they have to be good. Burgers are judged on taste, presentation, spirit, and showmanship. Hamburger plays a major part in the Great Bowls of Fire Chili Cook-off, as well. After all, what would a great bowl of chili be without hamburger meat and a few jalapeños?

A good American celebration almost requires a car and Harley show and this event's no exception. Vehicles on display range from a Conestoga wagon, cars from the

1920s and 1930s, red classic Thunderbirds, 'vettes, and Harley Road King motorcycles. Classic and hot rod clubs from the area help spread the word and supply many of the entries.

Throughout the event, artisans sell their wares while games and fun are supplied to keep the kids happy and entertained in a family-friendly atmosphere. After a day of eye-popping hamburgers, fiery chilis, swinging musical entertainment, and custom-designed wheels, everyone knows it's great to be alive.

In the evening, joyous music and other live entertainment fills the square with a variety of musical diversions. At night the square becomes an all-American stage, with everyone's feet tapping and heads bobbing in time to the rhythmic musical beat.

Athens, the seat of Henderson County, is located along Texas Highway 31 and U.S. Highway 175.

HOT VENISON CHILI

In a large Dutch oven, sauté all fresh vegetables in oil until tender. In separate skillet, brown venison and beef together. When no longer pink, drain fat and rinse with water. Add to vegetables. Add tomatoes, tomato paste, and seasonings. Let simmer over low heat for at least 2 hours. Add water as needed for desired consistency. Add beans 15 minutes before serving. Serve over rice or corn chips with shredded cheese, fresh onions, and chopped jalapeños.

Melinda McGowen
Conroe Courier Holiday Cookbook, prize winner
Conroe, Texas

3 onions: 2 finely chopped,
1 in large chunks

4 stalks celery, chopped

1 clove garlic, chopped

6 jalapeño peppers, chopped

1 tablespoon vegetable oil

1 pound venison, ground

1 pound round steak, ground

14$\frac{1}{2}$ ounces canned whole
tomatoes, undrained

10 ounces canned Rotel
tomatoes

6 ounces canned tomato paste

chili powder (to taste)

seasoned salt

fresh ground pepper

dash garlic powder

15 ounces canned pinto beans,
optional

shredded cheese, fresh onion,
chopped, and chopped
jalapeños for topping

ZESTY BASIL BURGERS

1 pound lean ground beef

3 tablespoons finely chopped onion

1 clove garlic, crushed

$^3/_4$ teaspoon salt

$^1/_4$ teaspoon pepper

4 crusty rolls, split

1 cup packed spinach leaves

4 tomato slices

Basil Mayonnaise

3 tablespoons reduced-calorie mayonnaise

1 tablespoon chopped fresh basil or 1 teaspoon dried basil leaves

1 teaspoon Dijon-style mustard

In medium bowl, combine ground beef, onion, garlic, salt, and pepper, mixing lightly but thoroughly. Shape into four oval, $^1/_2$-inch thick patties. Heat large, non-stick skillet over medium heat until hot. Place patties in skillet, cook 7 to 8 minutes, or until no longer pink and juices run clear, turning once. Meanwhile, in small bowl, combine Basil Mayonnaise ingredients and mix well. Line bottom half of each roll with spinach and tomato. Place burger on tomato, top with 1 tablespoon mayonnaise mixture. Close with top half of roll.

Texas Beef Council
Austin, Texas

GRILLED JALAPEÑO CHEESEBURGERS

In medium bowl, combine ground beef, jalapeño pepper, and Mexican seasoning, mixing lightly but thoroughly. Shape into four $1/2$-inch thick patties. Place patties on grid over medium, ash-covered coals. Grill, uncovered, 14 to 16 minutes or until centers are no longer pink, turning once. Approximately 1 minute before burgers are done, sprinkle each with 1 tablespoon cheese. Place one slice tomato on bottom half of each bun, top with burger and close sandwich.

Texas Beef Council
Austin, Texas

1 pound lean ground beef

2 teaspoons seeded, chopped jalapeño pepper

$1^1/_2$ teaspoons Mexican seasoning

$1/_4$ cup shredded Monterey Jack cheese

4 thin tomato slices

4 hamburger buns, split, toasted

PIÑATA BURGER

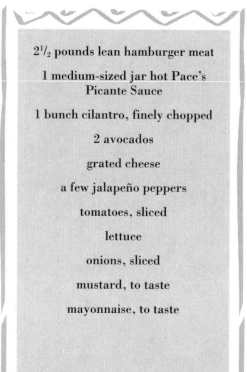

2¹/₂ pounds lean hamburger meat

1 medium-sized jar hot Pace's
Picante Sauce

1 bunch cilantro, finely chopped

2 avocados

grated cheese

a few jalapeño peppers

tomatoes, sliced

lettuce

onions, sliced

mustard, to taste

mayonnaise, to taste

Mix hamburger and picante sauce together thoroughly; shape into 2 patties. Place 4 slices of avocado, grated cheese, and a few jalapeños on top of one patty. Place second patty on the top and seal edges. Place on a charcoal grill. Do not turn over until thoroughly done on one side, approximately 10 minutes, then turn over and grill another 10 minutes. Cut proportionately and serve on homemade buns with tomato, lettuce, onions, mustard, and mayonnaise.

First National Bank
First Place winner
Athens, Texas

WATERMELON THUMP

LULING

Annual. Last Thursday, Friday, and Saturday in June.

Let's start with the basics. Picture this—you're in the market or at a produce stand checking out the seasonal watermelon supply. Do you select by appearance? Weight? Ripeness? Or do you thump? If your selection process includes the thump, then head for Luling and the annual Watermelon Thump.

In 1954, looking for a way to honor the growers and promote the Luling watermelon market, the principal of Luling Elementary School planted the seed to establish a watermelon celebration. The idea was nurtured, cultivated, and grew until it nearly burst with flavor and gusto.

The festival events are numerous. There's a Watermelon Thump Queen crowned each year, and she presides over the giant Watermelon Thump Parade, which starts promptly at 10 A.M. on Thump Saturday. Floats from far and wide participate, as well as local and military bands, Shriners, and clowns. Other highlights of the three-day event include a carnival, street dances, food booths with local specialties, a beer garden with continuous live entertainment, a children's stage, an exhibitors market, and a rodeo.

The thump-fest continues with a plethora of activities including a car rally, melon-eating contests, and the auction of the top melons. An arts-and-crafts exhibit and golf and bowling tournament round out the events. However, you'll want to save your energy for the really big showcase event.

Hundreds of dollars in cash prizes are awarded each year in the annual Seed-Spitting Contests. In 1981 a world record was set in Luling for the longest watermelon seed-spit. The record of 65 feet, 4 inches was set by a festival attendee from Houston. Then in 1989 a local man re-established the record, still standing at the time of this writing, by spitting a distance of 68 feet, $9^1/_8$ inches.

If you're twenty-one or older, you'll want to pick up the Luling Watermelon Thump Championship Seed-Spitting Official Rules. They'll provide you with instructions, the words to the official thump seed-spitting song, some helpful hints, and several seed-spitting yells to be performed by your friends and family. Heck, why not try it? You may be establishing the seed of a family tradition for generations to come.

Luling is planted about 55 miles northeast of San Antonio off Interstate 10. Website location: www.bcsnet.net/lulingcc

SPICED WATERMELON PIE

Preset oven to 450°. Remove the outer green part of the rind and most of the pulp from the watermelon and cut into ¼-inch cubes before measuring. Place the cubed rind in a medium saucepan and add water to cover. Bring to a boil and simmer until translucent and tender. Drain. Add sugar, cinnamon, cloves, nutmeg, raisins, pecans, salt, flour, and vinegar to cubes. Stir well. Pour the mixture into pastry shell; cover with top pastry crust, and cut steam vents. Bake at 450° until crust is slightly browned. Reduce temperature to 350° and bake until filling is set.

Georgie Morven
Recipes
National Watermelon Association

 This is a light, summertime, mincemeat pie.

2 cups cubed watermelon rind
(not pickled rind)

1 cup sugar

1 teaspoon ground cinnamon

¼ teaspoon ground cloves

¼ heaping teaspoon ground
nutmeg

½ cup raisins

½ cup chopped pecans

⅛ teaspoon salt

2 teaspoons flour

¼ cup cider or white vinegar

pie pastry for
2 9-inch crusts, uncooked

INDIVIDUAL BITE-SIZED SPICED WATERMELON PIES

Pastry

2 3-ounce packages cream cheese

1 cup margarine or butter

2 cups flour

Prepare filling the same as for Spiced Watermelon Pie (see previous recipe).

Mix all ingredients into a pastry dough, roll in a ball, and chill for 1 hour. Make into 1-inch balls and press to fit small, ungreased muffin tins. Fill each pastry with a scant teaspoon of pie filling. Bake at 350° for 25 to 30 minutes.

Luling Watermelon Thump Association
Luling, Texas

 These small pies are similar to pecan tassies with mincemeat filling.

SOUTHWESTERN STYLE WATERMELON SALAD

Mix together cumin, salt, cayenne, and chili powder. In serving bowl, toss together melon, cumin mixture, lime juice, and coriander or basil until well combined. Serve immediately.

Luling Watermelon Thump Association
Luling, Texas

$1/2$ teaspoon ground cumin

$1/2$ teaspoon salt (or to taste)

$1/8$ teaspoon cayenne
(or to taste)

$1/4$ teaspoon chili powder

4 cups watermelon pieces
($3/4$-inch cubes with seeds and
rind removed)

3 teaspoons fresh lime juice

2 teaspoons shredded fresh
coriander (or basil)

WATERMELON ICE CREAM PIE

1¹/₂ cups fine graham cracker crumbs

¹/₂ cup melted margarine

1 cup seedless watermelon chunks

1 quart softened vanilla ice cream

In medium bowl, mix together cracker crumbs and margarine. Press mixture into 9-inch pie plate. Refrigerate one hour. Place watermelon in blender or food processor container. Cover and blend on low speed for 30 seconds. Swirl mixture through ice cream. Firmly pack ice cream into crust. Cover and freeze several hours or until firm.

Luling Watermelon Thump Association
Luling, Texas

WATERMELON CAKE

Cake: Preheat oven to 350°. Grease and flour bundt pan. In a large bowl, mix all ingredients. Pour into bundt pan and bake about 35 minutes or until wooden pick inserted in cake comes out clean. When cool, ice with watermelon icing.

Icing: In a bowl, mix cream cheese and butter until fluffy. Add confectioners' sugar and watermelon juice; stir until blended.

Luling Watermelon Thump Association
Luling, Texas

Cake
1 box white cake mix

3 ounces packaged mixed-fruit gelatin

$1\frac{1}{3}$ cups seedless watermelon cubes

3 egg whites

1 tablespoon oil

icing (recipe follows)

Icing
6 ounces packaged cream cheese

$\frac{1}{4}$ cup butter

2 cups confectioners' sugar

$\frac{1}{4}$ cup watermelon juice

WESTERN HERITAGE CLASSIC RANCH RODEO

ABILENE

Annual. Second weekend in May.

There's not a rhinestone cowboy or cigarette model in the bunch as the folks in Abilene gather together at the Western Heritage Classic and Ranch Rodeo. What you'll find are real cowboys from working ranches across the United States competing in riding, roping, and cutting competitions. If you've ever longed to find out about ranch and cowboy life, this is the place to be.

If you feel compelled to wear your rhinestones, though, the Rhinestone Round-up kicks off the festivities with a dinner and art show. They're followed by the Ranch Rodeo and a dance. Don't forget your best boots . . . who knows, you may get a chance to show off those boot-scootin' lessons you've been taking.

During the festivities you'll hear some outstanding cowboy poetry, plenty of western music, and other entertainment. There are also sheep dog trials, cowboy matched horse races, the world's largest bit and spur show, and enough children's activities to keep them going for the weekend and then some.

A highlight of the event is the Chuck Wagon Cookoff where more than twenty-five chuck wagons from across Texas compete. The National Chuck Wagon Association sanctions the Chuck Wagon Cookoff. It's your chance to take a trip back in time. The traditions of the chuck wagon and open-range cooking are in evidence as wagons are displayed in the authentic style of the nineteenth-century trail-driving era. You'll discover historically dressed cooks and helpers preparing a traditional and unique style of cooking. All equipment, food, and campsites are presented as closely as possible to what they were like during trail-driving days.

Today, the chuck wagon remains a vital part of the cattle industry. It not only feeds working cowboys on larger ranches, but it's also a social gathering place during cowboy celebrations, fairs, meetings, and other important events.

Abilene is located in the east-west center of the state along Interstate 20. The annual Western Heritage Classic is held at the Taylor County Expo Center on Texas Highway 36. Website location: www.abilene.com/visitors

VACA LOCA LASAGNE

1 pound pinto beans

garlic to taste

cumin to taste

chili powder to taste

2 cups salsa

12 corn tortillas

1 container nonfat ricotta cheese or tofu

16 ounces salsa, hot or mild, depending on your toughness

nonfat yogurt, optional

Cook beans as instructed on package, adding garlic, cumin, and chili powder. Mash cooked pinto beans. Spoon a couple spoonfuls of salsa on the bottom of an 8 x 12-inch casserole. Cover with tortillas and spread on a layer of mashed beans. Spoon on more salsa, cover with tortillas, add a layer of ricotta or tofu, and spoon on more salsa. Add another layer of tortillas and beans, and then yogurt and salsa. Bake at 350° for about 30 minutes.

Ray Finfer, Creator
Death by Chili
Irving, Texas

 Serve with Mexican rice and a green salad.

FIESTA BEEF STEAKS

Sprinkle both sides of beef steaks with lime juice. Wrap tortillas securely in heavy-duty aluminum foil. Place steaks on grid over medium, ash-covered coals. Grill, uncovered, 12 to 14 minutes for medium-rare to medium doneness, turning occasionally. Place tortilla packet on outer edge of grid and heat 5 minutes, turning once. Trim fat from steaks; season with salt and pepper, if desired. Serve with salsa and tortillas.

Texas Beef Council
Austin, Texas

4 beef rib eye steaks, cut 1-inch thick

2 tablespoons fresh lime juice

8 small flour tortillas

salt and pepper to taste

1 cup prepared chunky salsa

MEXICALI PORK CHOPS WITH BLACK BEANS

15 ounces canned black beans, rinsed and drained

1 cup salsa or picante sauce

4 ounces canned chopped green chilies, undrained

1 tablespoon chopped fresh cilantro

2 teaspoons chili powder

1/4 teaspoon pepper

4 boneless pork chops, 3/4-inch thick

vegetable oil

sour cream, optional

In a medium bowl, combine black beans, salsa or picante sauce, chilies, cilantro, chili powder, and pepper. Set aside. Heat a large skillet over medium-high heat. Brush chops lightly with oil and brown on each side; remove chops. Add bean mixture to skillet and bring to a boil. Return chops to skillet and cover tightly, and cook over low heat for 5 to 6 minutes or until chops are done. Serve with bean mixture. Top with sour cream if desired.

National Pork Producers Council
Des Moines, Iowa

WINE AND FOOD FESTIVAL

SAN ANGELO

Annual. Usually in April.

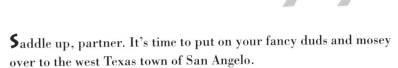

Saddle up, partner. It's time to put on your fancy duds and mosey over to the west Texas town of San Angelo.

What could be better than spending a weekend strolling along the banks and trails of the beautiful Concho River, soaking in the rays of the warm spring sun? Here's your chance to spend two days enjoying the world of family, friends, wine, and food. It's all available during the annual Texas Wine and Food Festival held in San Angelo.

Each year the San Angelo Cultural Affairs Council hosts this chance to sample some of the best food and wine Texas has to offer. The events and activities are plentiful. The action commences on Friday with a formal and elegant gourmet dinner beginning at 7 P.M. Each year an acclaimed guest chef presents a multi-course meal plus hors d'oeuvres in an elegant West Texas setting. As an attendee, you're invited to participate in a silent auction featuring fine wines and spirits, specialty foods, and one-of-a-kind offerings.

On Saturday the festival program includes celebrity-chef cooking classes. Not only will you observe the preparation of several signature dishes, but the chefs often distribute their special recipes to those participating in the culinary sessions. You'll discover several programs offering seminars by vintners and authorities regarding Texas wines suitable for pairing and cooking.

Saturday concludes with an outdoor evening event known as the Wine, Brew and Food Tasting Finale. That's where participants may purchase tickets to sample epicurean delights offered by many of the best Texas vintners, celebrity chefs, restaurants, caterers, and breweries. Throughout the night, live entertainment creates an unforgettable experience with a unique West Texas flavor. The fashionable finale takes place within walking distance of the Concho River, San Angelo Museum of Fine Arts, and the Fort Concho National Historic Landmark.

The Texas Wine and Food Festival serves as the primary fundraiser for the San Angelo Cultural Affairs Council. The council supports arts and cultural activities in San Angelo and the Concho Valley.

San Angelo is filled with dozens of destination attractions. The city is located where U.S. Highways 67 and 87 intersect.

All recipes for this section contributed by Texas wine experts Thomas and Gina Castle, authors of *Touring Texas Wineries.*

COWBOY CAVIAR

Soak beans in wine for 30 minutes. Drain; mix together with onion, garlic, oil, olives, lime juice, and black pepper. Cover and refrigerate 2 hours. Cool and peel eggs; separate the whites from yolks, taking care not to cut into the yolks. Set the yolks aside, chop the egg whites into small pieces, and refrigerate both. Dice the fresh tomato and set aside.

To serve, spread cream cheese on a plate, spoon on bean mix evenly, and place diced tomato in the center of the plate, forming a small hill. Surround the tomato with a ring of picante sauce, then surround the picante sauce with a ring of egg whites, filling the plate to the edge. Grate or finely chop 2 of the egg yolks and sprinkle around the plate. Place third egg yolk in the center of tomato. Serve immediately with tortilla chips or crackers.

 This easy-to-prepare appetizer will be a sure hit at your next party and goes well with any wine you like. Numerous versions of this recipe have been circulated over the past decade, but this one adds Texas wine and a few twists.

15 ounces canned black beans, rinsed & drained

3 to 4 ounces Cap*Rock Winery's Muscat Canelli

1 medium onion, finely chopped

3 cloves garlic, finely chopped

2 tablespoons olive oil

4 ounces canned ripe olives, drained and finely chopped

3 tablespoons lime juice

black pepper to taste

3 hard-boiled eggs

1 tomato

8 ounces packaged cream cheese

1 10- to 15-ounce bottle mild picante sauce

tortilla chips or crackers

BUBBLING GRILLED CHICKEN

5 ounces Ste. Genevieve
White Zinfandel

16 ounces canned chicken
broth

8 ounces bottled Italian
salad dressing

$1/2$ cup lemon juice

$1/2$ medium onion, chopped

4 cloves garlic, chopped

2 tablespoons chopped
fresh cilantro

non-stick vegetable oil
spray

2 to 3 pounds boneless
chicken breasts, skinned

In bowl, combine wine, chicken broth, Italian dressing, lemon juice, onion, garlic, and cilantro, mixing thoroughly to create sauce. Spray large aluminum roasting pan (like turkey pan at local grocery store) with non-stick vegetable oil, place chicken breasts in pan, and pour in sauce. The sauce should cover the chicken; if not, add White Zinfandel. Cover with aluminum foil and place on 350° grill. Check temperature and sauce level regularly. Maintain temperature at 350°. There should be $1/2$ inch of broth in the pan at all times; add White Zinfandel if sauce is reduced too quickly. Depending on the grill's heat, cooking time will average 30 to 50 minutes. Remove the cover for last 5 to 10 minutes for extra flavor.

While this dish is cooking, try combining the White Zinfandel with ice and Sprite for a refreshing wine cooler as you sit back and watch the grill. This dish goes well with Llano Estacado Chenin Blanc, or an optional tasting of 2 to 3 Texas Chardonnays.

JOLTED BAR-B-QUE CHICKEN

Place all ingredients in a slow-cooker. Cook on low heat 6 to 7 hours, or high heat for 2 to 3 hours. Serve the chicken by cutting into serving-sized pieces placed on a platter of white rice. Spoon a generous portion of the broth onto the platter for extra flavor. Accompany with fresh vegetables or a three-bean salad.

A Texas Muscat Canelli or Chenin Blanc goes well with this meal. This fun recipe is almost too good to be true as a slow-cooker dish—the chicken has that cooked-outdoors flavor. The sweetness of the wine, ketchup, and Coca Cola combine to create a marvelous barbecue-style sauce, easy to prepare and a snap to clean up after.

1 4-pound fresh whole chicken, cleaned

1 small bottle of ketchup

4 ounces Llano Estacado Chenin Blanc

1 can Coca Cola

salt and pepper to taste

$\frac{1}{4}$ cup lemon juice

WASHINGTON-ON-THE-BRAZOS BRISKET

Uncle Lester's Barbecue Sauce

1 cup barbecue sauce

4 tablespoons mustard

1 lemon, quartered

2 cloves garlic, minced

3 tablespoons molasses

1 ounce Cap*Rock Garnet Royale

Brisket Sealing Paste

1 cup flour

3 tablespoons mustard, horseradish based

1 12- to 15-pound brisket, trimmed

salt and pepper

Combine the ingredients of Uncle Lester's Barbecue Sauce in bowl, mixing thoroughly. Squeeze the lemon to release juice, then drop into the sauce. Let stand until needed. Combine the Sealing Paste ingredients, slowly adding the flour to prevent lumps from forming. Season the brisket with salt and pepper and brush on the Sealing Paste, completely covering the brisket. Wrap brisket in aluminum foil and place on grill with the foil seam easily accessible. After cooking 3 to 4 hours, apply generous layer of Uncle Lester's Barbecue Sauce over the brisket every 30 minutes until brisket is tender.

Serve this hearty meal with a Fall Creek Vineyards Granite Reserve.

WORLD'S LARGEST RATTLE-SNAKE ROUND-UP

SWEETWATER

Annual. Second weekend in March.

45

You never thought you'd eat one. Right?

For more than 40 years, the Sweetwater Jaycees have brought to West Texas this festival of international proportion that gets worldwide media coverage. It's your chance to help celebrate the American reptile with a rattle on the end of its tail. Don't worry—rattlers usually send out a warning sound before they strike.

The event began as an effort to rid the town of rattlers, once in abundance in the Sweetwater area. The event grew rapidly over the years and now over 100 tons of the Western Diamondback snakes have been harvested.

There's plenty to do at this unique celebration that currently attracts 30,000 visitors. They (the visitors, not the snakes) come from all fifty states, Europe, Asia, and North and South America. Rattlers eat birds and small mammals. Now's your chance to turn the tables on the critter named for the diamond-shaped blotches that cover its body. If you've ever wondered what rattlesnake meat tastes like, here's an opportunity to find out.

With tongue in cheek, and rattles in hand, you can view the Rattlesnake Parade held in the middle of town. It features plenty of talented bands, decorated floats, antique cars, and contestants competing for Miss Snake Charmer. The beauties vying for the queen title have an opportunity to win scholarship money donated by the Jaycees.

Just in case you run across a live one, demonstrations are held by professional snake handlers who, with viper in hand, provide educational and entertaining safety demonstrations. Who knows, afterwards you may find yourself filled with emotion and ready to take on the care and survival of the species. Since rattlesnake venom is an important part of medical research, trained snake handlers demonstrate the removal of venom from live rattlesnakes and allow you to watch.

On Saturday of the Round-Up, the cook-off attracts hundreds of cooks and thousands of spectators. You can join the cooks as they prepare chicken, beans, pork ribs, brisket, and chili taste sensations. The cook-off is held adjacent to the rattlesnake displays. If you want, come back Sunday afternoon to participate in the snake-meat-eating contest. If you're smitten with the taste of the meat, guided snake hunts occur on Friday, Saturday, and Sunday. Pack up your hand mirror, high-top boots, and snakebite kit, and join the crowd.

Sweetwater is located on U.S. Highway 84, less than 50 miles west of Abilene. Oh, yeah . . . you need a Texas hunting license to bag your own snake!

RATTLESNAKE

Take the rattlesnake and lay it on a cutting board. Remove head plus at least 2 inches into the body in order to remove all poisons. Then run a knife along the belly of the snake (the skin comes off quite easily). Clean out the inside of the snake and cut into about 3-inch pieces. Freeze these overnight. When ready to prepare, remove from freezer. Allow to thaw slightly. Dip in egg, then in breading mix. Deep-fat fry for 20 minutes in fat heated to 300°. The meat is similar to chicken or frog legs but very boney. Eat by picking the meat off the bones.

Joyce LaFray
Country Cookin' cookbook
St. Petersburg, Florida

 "No wonder rattlesnake hunts are so popular! Unless you are an expert rattlesnake hunter, we advise you *not* to hunt your own."

1 rattlesnake

1 egg, beaten

breading mix

oil or Crisco for frying

SWEETWATER RATTLESNAKE

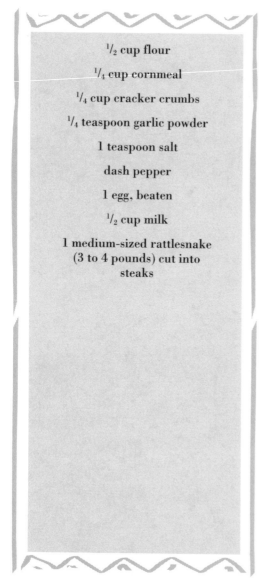

½ cup flour

¼ cup cornmeal

¼ cup cracker crumbs

¼ teaspoon garlic powder

1 teaspoon salt

dash pepper

1 egg, beaten

½ cup milk

1 medium-sized rattlesnake
(3 to 4 pounds) cut into
steaks

Mix flour, cornmeal, cracker crumbs, garlic powder, salt, and pepper in a bag. Add beaten egg to milk and dip snake steaks. Coat the steaks by adding them to the bag. Place in small amount of cooking oil that has been heated to 400° and cook, uncovered, until brown or until meat floats in oil.

Recipe courtesy Sweetwater Chamber of Commerce
Sweetwater, Texas

Deep-Fried Rattlesnake

Marinate in sweet milk for 2 hours. Dredge in cornmeal, or bread crumbs, or a combination of both. Deep-fat fry until brown. Serve with Louisiana Hot Sauce, Texas Pepper Sauce, or tartar sauce.

Sweetwater Chamber of Commerce
Sweetwater, Texas

Kill it

Remove the head; suspend by
tail for 1 hour

Skin; gut

Chop into chunks

cornmeal or bread crumbs

RATTLESNAKE SALAD

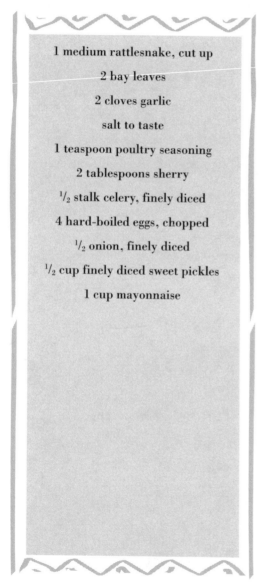

1 medium rattlesnake, cut up

2 bay leaves

2 cloves garlic

salt to taste

1 teaspoon poultry seasoning

2 tablespoons sherry

$\frac{1}{2}$ stalk celery, finely diced

4 hard-boiled eggs, chopped

$\frac{1}{2}$ onion, finely diced

$\frac{1}{2}$ cup finely diced sweet pickles

1 cup mayonnaise

Combine first 5 ingredients and boil until meat is tender. Chop meat finely and mix well with remaining ingredients. Serve on sandwiches or over quartered tomatoes and lettuce.

Uncle Phaedrus
phaedrus@ebicom.net

SOUTHERN FRIED RATTLESNAKE

Skin rattlesnake; clean and wash meat. Cut into 4-inch pieces. Beat egg and milk together. Mix salt, pepper, garlic salt, Accent, and flour. Preheat deep-fat fryer with cooking oil. Dip snake into egg mixture, then in flour mixture, and place it in hot oil. Cook until golden brown.

Submitted via E-mail from C.C. Cheney, California

 Don't knock it until you've tried it.

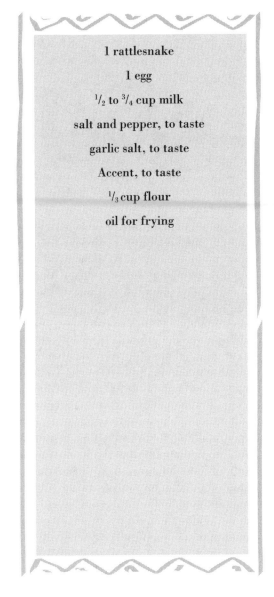

1 rattlesnake

1 egg

$1/2$ to $3/4$ cup milk

salt and pepper, to taste

garlic salt, to taste

Accent, to taste

$1/3$ cup flour

oil for frying

WURSTFEST

NEW BRAUNFELS

Annual. Late October.

Pretzels, polka music, sausage, strudel, and suds—that's what the Wurstfest is all about. Since 1961 members of the Wurstfest Association have celebrated New Braunfels' German heritage and the making of sausage with a ten-day event. "Why go?" you ask? A quick rundown will likely get your travel and culinary juices flowing.

GREAT FOOD. Sausage, sauerkraut, kartoffel puffers, strudel, bratwurst, knackwurst, bread pudding, funnel cakes, pretzels, pastries, and plenty more.

GREAT MUSIC. More than sixty different groups perform. You'll hear everything from Alpine horns to polka music. The massive Wursthalle and two large tents showcase some of the finest entertainers in the world.

GREAT FUN. Consistently rated as one of the top events in North America, Wurstfest is designed for the entire family. In addition to great music and food, there's an annual Heritage Exhibit, a melodrama, arts and crafts, a walk and run, a bicycle classic, a regatta, and a Hummel Museum exhibit.

Folks who attend the Wurstfest experience German culture by selecting from more than 100 types of food, listening to plenty of German music, and participating in a number of family activities such as historical tours, Children's Museum adventures, art shows, theater performances, and plenty of chances for dance lovers to scoot their boots. If you're a Hummel fancier, you're invited to take part in the Hummel Look-Alike Contest. Adults and children are asked to select a favorite Hummel figurine and dress accordingly.

The event organizers invite you to salute the sausage during this dynamic celebration. After all, it's where the best of times are the "wurst" of times. The Wurstfest grounds are located just inside Landa Park along the banks of the beautiful Comal River. The park's situated near the intersection of Landa Park Drive and Landa Street.

New Braunfels is located off Interstate 35, approximately 40 miles south of Austin and 20 miles north of San Antonio. Website location: www.new-braunfels.com/wurstfest

All recipes in this section contributed by the Wurstfest Association of New Braunfels.

ROTKRAUT

1 large red cabbage

salt and pepper to taste

2 tablespoons lard or shortening

$^1/_2$ cup tarragon vinegar

$^1/_2$ cup red wine

3 tablespoons sugar

3 tablespoons water

2 tart apples, sliced

2 tablespoons red currant jelly

$^1/_2$ teaspoon powdered cloves

$^1/_2$ teaspoon caraway seeds

Remove stem and outside leaves from cabbage, shred, and dust with salt and pepper. In an enamel saucepan, melt lard or shortening, add cabbage, and sprinkle with vinegar. With a wooden spoon, stir and press down cabbage over low heat and cook without adding more liquid, if possible. Add $^1/_2$ cup red wine, if necessary. In small skillet, dissolve sugar in 3 tablespoons water and cook the syrup until brown. Add caramel to cabbage and cover pan. Simmer cabbage for 1$^1/_2$ hours. Add apples, currant jelly, cloves, and caraway seeds. Simmer cabbage for 20 minutes more, drain, and serve at once.

BARBECUED SPARERIBS

Arrange ribs and onions in large baking pan. Season with salt and pepper. Brown both sides under an oven broiler. In small piece of cheesecloth, tie bay leaf, cloves, mixed spices, and thyme. Add this bouquet garni to pan along with the carrots. Mix mustard, garlic, vinegar, sugar, chili sauce, and Worcestershire sauce. Pour mix over ribs. Add enough stock or bouillon to barely cover. Roast in moderate 350° oven about 1^1/$_2$ hours or until done.

6 pounds pork spareribs

2 medium onions, quartered

1 teaspoon salt

^{1}/$_4$ teaspoon pepper

1 bay leaf

3 cloves

^{1}/$_2$ teaspoon mixed spices

^{1}/$_8$ teaspoon thyme

2 carrots, sliced thin

1 teaspoon prepared mustard

1 clove garlic, mashed

^{1}/$_4$ cup vinegar

^{1}/$_4$ cup sugar

3 cups chili sauce

1 tablespoon Worcestershire sauce

stock or bouillon

GERMAN SHORT RIBS OF BEEF

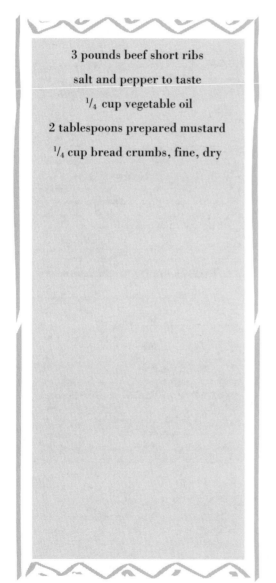

3 pounds beef short ribs

salt and pepper to taste

$1/4$ cup vegetable oil

2 tablespoons prepared mustard

$1/4$ cup bread crumbs, fine, dry

Wipe meat with paper towel and season with salt and pepper. Place in shallow roasting pan. Bake in oven at 350° until tender. Baste with pan juices often. Divide into serving pieces and coat with mixture of oil and mustard. Sprinkle with bread crumbs and place under broiler until brown.

BLACK FOREST TORTE

Black Forest Torte: Beat egg yolks with sugar until mixture is thick and light. Fold in walnuts, bread crumbs, and apples. Beat egg whites until stiff but not dry. Fold into batter. Pour batter into buttered 8-inch springform pan. Bake in moderate 350° oven for 45 minutes. Cool torte in pan and remove. Frost with whipped cream. Decorate with chopped walnuts or confectioners' sugar. Serve with Butterscotch Rum Sauce.

Butterscotch Rum Sauce: Combine the cream, brown sugar, and sweet butter and bring to a boil. Boil the syrup vigorously for about 3 minutes or until it is thick. Remove from heat, let cool for 5 minutes, then stir in the rum. Serve with Black Forest Torte.

Black Forest Torte

3 eggs, separated

$^1/_2$ cup sugar

$1^1/_4$ cups finely chopped walnuts

$^1/_4$ cup bread crumbs

2 medium apples, grated

1 cup heavy cream, whipped (sweeten to taste)

chopped walnuts or confectioners' sugar for decoration

Butterscotch Rum Sauce (recipe follows)

Butterscotch Rum Sauce

$^1/_2$ cup light cream

$1^1/_2$ cups brown sugar

3 tablespoons sweet butter

$^1/_4$ cup light rum

YAMBOREE

GILMER

Annual. Four days in October.

So much goes on at the East Texas Yamboree, its souvenir program contains over seventy pages. The Yamboree has been held annually since 1935, with the exception of a two-year period during World War II. Throughout the years, the Yamboree has grown from a local event to one that draws a crowd of nearly one hundred thousand people.

You're guaranteed a near-perfect round-up of food, games, arts and crafts, exhibits, activities for kids, entertainment, and animals. Although the crowds grow every year, you'll find Yamboree festival organizers manage to keep its small-town flavor.

The roster of activities is as varied as the people who attend. Here's a kaleidoscopic look at some impressive happenings that capture the festival's spirit and atmosphere.

Queen's Coronation and Pageant
Home Canning Competition
Street and Barn Dances
Art and Photography Show
Livestock Show
Carnival
Yam Pie Contest & Judging
School/Youth Parade
"Tater Trot" 10K Run
Decorated Yam Contest

Antique and Classic Car Show and
  Parade
Fiddlers' Contest
Intra-County Barbecue
Marching Bands
Rabbit Show
Steer Judging
Golf Tournament
"Tour de Yam" Bicycle Tours

This tribute to the yam is one giant party attended by thousands of fun-loving celebrants. The Yamboree's so large, in fact, individual event locations include Yamboree Park, Courthouse Square, Gilmer High School Stadium, and the Civic Center.

Make it a family affair. The Yamboree offers a chance to sample regional cuisine, meet fascinating people, and share some Texas hospitality and traditions. It's four days of pure cowboy fun for the entire family. Who knows, you may even find an answer to the age-old question, "What's the difference between a yam and a sweet potato?" Whatever your pleasure, you'll go home happy. After all, isn't that what a party's for?

Gilmer and Yamboree Park are found along U.S. Highway 271, east of Dallas.

YAM PIE

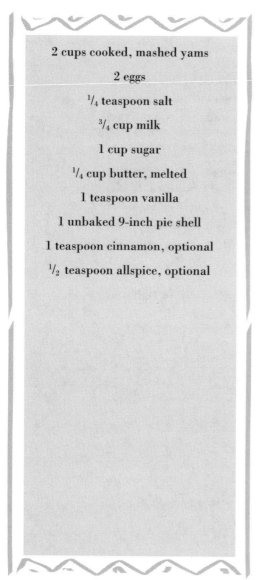

2 cups cooked, mashed yams

2 eggs

$^1/_4$ teaspoon salt

$^3/_4$ cup milk

1 cup sugar

$^1/_4$ cup butter, melted

1 teaspoon vanilla

1 unbaked 9-inch pie shell

1 teaspoon cinnamon, optional

$^1/_2$ teaspoon allspice, optional

Mix all ingredients; pour into unbaked pie shell. Bake at 350°for 1 hour. May add 1 teaspoon cinnamon and $^1/_2$ teaspoon allspice to ingredients, if desired.

East Texas Yamboree Committee
Gilmer, Texas

GLAZED YAMS

Cook yams 10 minutes in boiling water. Pare. Cut in half lengthwise and place in casserole. Make a syrup by boiling sugar and water 3 minutes, add butter, and pour over yams. Bake at 375°, basting frequently until yams are tender. An hour or more is usually required.

Glenda Asbury
Dallas, Texas

6 yams

salt and pepper to taste

$^1/_2$ cup brown sugar

$^1/_4$ cup water

$^1/_4$ cup butter

CANDIED YAMS

2 to 3 whole yams

¼ cup butter or margarine

¼ cup brown sugar

mini-marshmallows

Wash yams, prick with fork, and microwave until tender. Peel and dice yams; place in casserole baking dish. Melt butter or margarine in small saucepan, add brown sugar, pour over yams, and mix gently. Bake at 350° for 15 to 20 minutes. Add marshmallows to taste and stir to mix. Marshmallows will melt slightly. Sprinkle marshmallows on top to garnish and serve.

Al Sabot
Paris, Texas

PORK AND YAM PIE

Sauté onions and garlic in butter. Add parsley, green pepper, and meat. Cook until meat has lost its raw look. Add salt, pepper, and tomato juice. Simmer, covered, for 45 minutes. Remove from heat and add capers, raisins, and wine. Meanwhile, boil the yams until tender. Mash, adding butter, egg, and baking powder. Line a 9-inch, greased pie pan with half the yam mixture, pressing it down. Fill with meat mixture. Add remaining yam mixture. Bake at 350° for 35 to 45 minutes.

Paul Madden
Dallas, Texas

 Serve with steamed spinach or a green salad.

2 onions, finely chopped

2 cloves garlic, crushed

1 tablespoon butter

2 tablespoons chopped fresh parsley

1 green pepper, chopped

1 pound lean pork or turkey, ground

salt and pepper to taste

$1/2$ cup tomato juice

2 tablespoons capers

3 tablespoons raisins

4 tablespoons sherry or port

2 pounds yams, peeled

1 tablespoon butter

1 egg, slightly beaten

1 teaspoon baking powder

FURTHER FEASTINGS

The following selected events are among the many held in Texas annually. To obtain a complimentary copy of the quarterly *Texas Events Calendar*, write P.O. Box 5064, Austin, Texas, 78763-5064, or call 800-8888-TEX. To receive information regarding special events and festivals held in each community, write or call the city chamber of commerce and/or visitor center.

January

Make a Wish of Amarillo Chili Cookoff (Amarillo), 806-352-8783

Taste of the Island & Health Fair (South Padre Island), 210-761-6433, 800-SOPADRE

Wine and Chocolate Fantasia (Llano), 806-745-2258

February

Food and Wine Classic (Corpus Christi), 512-855-2213

Livestock and Rodeo Show Barbecue Cook Off (Houston), 713-791-9000

St. Michael's Sausage Lovers Festival (Levelland), 806-894-3157

South Texas Ranching Heritage Festival (Kingsville), 800-333-5032

March

Cork and Fork Affair—A Taste of Lubbock (Lubbock), 800-692-4035

Crawfish and Saltwater Crab Festival (Orange), 409-735-4152

Montgomery County Barbecue Cookoff (Conroe), 800-283-6646

Oysterfest (Fulton), 512-729-2388, 800-242-0071

Spamarama (Austin), 512-478-0098, 800-926-2282

Taste of Gumbo (Port Arthur), 409-727-8871

Taste of the Valley (Pharr), 210-968-3141

April

Apple Blossom Celebration (Idalou), 806-765-6772, 806-763-4666, 800-792-4035

Easter Festival, Chili Classic, & 5K Run (Kerrville), 830-257-3992, 830-367-4868

Fiesta San Antonio (San Antonio), 210-227-5191, 800-447-3372

Firemen's Extravaganza (Elgin), 512-285-4515

Houston International Festival (Houston), 713-654-8808, 800-365-7575

Main Street: Fort Worth Arts Festival (Fort Worth), 817-336-8791, 800-433-5747

New Vintage Wine & Food Festival (Grapevine), 817-424-0570

RioFest (Harlingen), 956-412-ARTS

Texas State Championship Fiddlers' Frolic (Hallettsville), 512-798-2311

Wild Game Cook-Off (Beaumont), 409-832-3432

May

Crawfish Festival (Beaumont), 409-880-3749, 800-392-4401

Crawfish Festival (Commerce), 903-886-2111

Founders Day Celebration (Emory), 903-473-2465

Kerrville Folk Festival (Kerrville), 830-257-3600

Old West Chuckwagon Dinner and Campfire Concert (Levelland), 806-894-3157

Rabbit Fest (Copperas Cove), 254-547-7571

Stagecoach BBQ Cookoff (Marshall), 903-935-7868

Shrimp on the Barbie Cook-off (South Padre Island), 210-761-6433, 800-SOPADRE

Texas Crab Festival (Crystal Beach), 409-684-5940

Viva! Cinco de Mayo (San Marcos), 512-396-2495

June

Dairy Day in Dallas (Dallas), 214-904-3050

Chisholm Trail Roundup, Trailblazer X BBQ Cook-Off (Ft. Worth), 800-433-5747

Fort Griffin Fandangle (Albany), 915-762-3838

Onion Festival (Noonday), 903-825-3584

Pecos Cantaloupe Festival (Pecos), 915-445-2406

Tigua St. Anthony's Day (El Paso), 915-859-3916

Tom-Tom Festival (Yoakum), 512-293-2309

July

Early Settlers Day Food and Music Festival (Levelland), 806-894-3157

Hot Burrito and Bluegrass Festival (Levelland), 806-894-3157

The Great Texas Mosquito Festival (Clute), 409-265-8392

Watermelon Festival (Hempstead), 409-826-8217

August

Austin Chronicle Hot Sauce Contest (Austin), 512-478-0098, 800-926-2282

Chili Super Bowl (Buffalo Gap), 915-675-8412

International Barbecue Cookoff (Taylor), 512-352-6364

XIT Rodeo & Reunion (Dalhart), 806-249-5646

September

Bartlett Volunteer Fire Department BBQ Cook-Off (Bartlett), 817-527-3333

Chili Superbowl Cookoff (Abilene), 915-677-2781

Grapefest (Grapevine), 817-424-0570

Kolache Festival (Caldwell), 409-567-3218

National Championship Indian Powwow (Grand Prairie), 214-647-2331

Rib Ticklin' Affair (Austin), 512-440-4036

Wine & Music Festival (Kerrville), 830-257-3600

World Championship Barbecue Goat Cookoff & Arts and Crafts Fair (Brady), 915-597-3491 (held the Saturday before Labor Day)

October

Autumn Trails (Winnsboro), 903-342-3666

Country Fest (Mt. Vernon), 903-537-4365

Czhilispiel Czech/German Festival (Flatonia), 512-865-3920

Food & Wine Fest (Fredericksburg), 830-997-8515

Keller Wild West Days (Keller), 817-431-2169

Oktoberfest (Round Top), 409-278-3530

Original International Tolbert/Fowler Memorial Championship Chili Cookoff (Terlingua), 903-874-5601

Punkin Days (Floydada), 806-983-3434

Seafair (Rockport), 800-242-0071

State Chili Championship & Ball (Fredericksburg), 210-997-6523

Taste of the Triangle (Beaumont), 409-880-3749, 800-392-4401

Wine and Clay Festival (Llano), 806-745-2258

World Championship Shrimp Cook-off (South Padre Island), 210-761-5433, 800-SOPADRE

November

Gathering of the Clans (Salado), 817-947-5040

Heritage Syrup Festival (Henderson), 903-657-5528

December

Candelight Posada (McAllen), 210-682-2871

Fiestas Navidenas in El Mercado (San Antonio), 210-207-8600

Krist Kindl Market (Copperas Cove), 254-547-7571

INFORMATION DIRECTORY

For information and details regarding special events, restaurants, lodging, shopping, and attractions contact the following:

Alley Oop Chili & BBQ Cookoff, Iraan
Iraan Chamber of Commerce, 509 West Sixth Street, P.O. Box 153, Iraan 79744; 915-739-2232.

Apple Butter Festival, Idalou
Apple Butter Festival, Apple Country, 505 32nd Street, Lubbock 79404; 806-765-6772.

Lubbock Visitors and Conventions Bureau, 14th and Avenue K, P.O. Box 561, Lubbock 79408; 806-763-4666, 800-692-4035.

Bar-B-Q Festival, Vidor
Vidor Chamber of Commerce, P.O. Box 413, Vidor 77662; 409-769-6339.

Black-Eyed Pea Jamboree, Athens
Athens Convention and Visitors Bureau, P.O. Box 2600, Athens 75751; 903-675-5818.

Blueberry Festival, Nacogdoches County
Nacogdoches County Chamber of Commerce, 513 North Street, Nacogdoches 75961; 409-560-5533.

Border Folk Festival, El Paso
Chamizal National Memorial, Festival Coordinator, 800 South Marcial, El Paso 79905; 915-532-7273, extension 102.

El Paso Civic Convention and Tourism Department, One Civic Center Plaza, El Paso 79901; 915-534-0696, 800-351-6024.

Butterfield Stage Days, Bridgeport
Bridgeport Chamber of Commerce, 1107 Eighth Street, Bridgeport 76426; 904-683-2076

Charro Days, Brownsville
Brownsville Convention and Visitors Bureau, P.O. Box 4697, Brownsville 78523; 210-546-3721, 800-626-2639.

Chilympiad, San Marcos
Republic of Texas Chilympiad Committee, P.O. Box 188, San Marcos 78667; 512-396-5400.

San Marcos Convention and Visitors Bureau, P.O. Box 2310, San Marcos 78667-2310; 512-353-3435, 888-200-5620.

Citrus Fiesta, Mission
Citrus Fiesta, 1600 Kika De La Garza, Mission 78573; 956-585-9724.

Mission Chamber of Commerce, 220 East 9th Street, Mission 78572; 956-585-2727.

Corn Festival, Holland
Holland Area Chamber of Commerce, P.O. Box 338, Holland 76534-0338; 254-657-2460.

Cotton Pickin' Fair & Go Texan Days, Hillsboro
Hillsboro Convention and Visitors Bureau, P.O. Box 358, Hillsboro 76645; 817-582-3100; 800-445-5726.

Crawfish Festival, Mauriceville
Mauriceville Crawfish Association, P.O. Box 683, Mauriceville 77626; 409-745-1202.

Dairy Festival & Ice Cream Freeze-off, Sulphur Springs
Sulphur Springs Tourism and Visitors Bureau, P.O. Box 347, Sulphur Springs 75483; 888-300-6623.

Fall Festival & World Champion Stew Contest, Hopkins County
Hopkins County Fall Festival Association, P.O. Box 177, Sulphur Springs, Texas 75483; 903-885-8071.

Fiery Foods Show, Austin
Dos Habaneros Shows, P.O. Box 629, Seguin 78156-0629; 830-379-2181.

Austin Convention and Visitors Bureau, 201 East 2nd Street, Austin 78701; 512-478-0098, 800-926-2282.

Folklife Festival, San Antonio
University of Texas, Institute of Texan Cultures, 801 South Bowie Street, San Antonio 78205-3296; 210-458-2257

San Antonio Convention and Visitors Bureau, 121 Alamo Plaza, P.O. Box 2277, San Antonio 78298; 210-270-8700, 800-447-3372.

General Granbury's Birthday Party and Bean Cook-Off, Granbury
Granbury Convention and Visitors Bureau, 100 North Crockett, Granbury 76048; 817-573-5548, 800-950-2212.

General Sam Houston Folk Festival, Huntsville
Huntsville Visitors and Convention Bureau, P.O. Box 538, Huntsville 77342-0538; 409-295-8113, 800-289-0389.

Germanfest, Muenster
Muenster Chamber of Commerce, P.O. Box 479, Muenster 76252; 817-759-2227.

Hill Country Wine & Food Festival, Austin
Hill Country Wine & Food Festival, 1006 Mopac Circle, Suite 102, Austin 78746; 512-329-0770.

International Apple Festival, Medina
Apple Festival Coordinator, P.O. Box 125, Medina 78055; 210-589-7224.

International Gumbo Cook-off, Orange
Greater Orange Area Chamber of Commerce, 1012 Green Avenue, Orange 77630; 409-883-3536.

Jalapeño Festival, Laredo
Laredo Convention and Visitors Bureau, P.O. Box 579, Laredo 78042; 210-795-2200, 800-361-3360.

Mex-Tex Menudo Cook Off, Midland
Midland Hispanic Chamber of Commerce, 1410 North Lamesa, P.O. Box 11134, Midland 79702; 915-682-2960, 915-683-3807.

Oktoberfest, Fredericksburg
Oktoberfest, P.O. Box 2222, Fredericksburg 78624; 830-997-4810.

Onion Festival, Weslaco
Weslaco Area Chamber of Commerce and Tourism Center, 1710 East Pike Boulevard, P.O. Box 8398, Weslaco 78599; 956-968-2102, 888-968-2102.

Peach Festival, Weatherford
Weatherford Chamber of Commerce, P.O. Box 310, Weatherford 76086; 817-596-3801.

Peach JAMboree & Rodeo, Stonewall
Stonewall Chamber of Commerce, P.O. Box 1, Stonewall 78671; 210-644-2735.

Pecan Festival, Groves
Groves Chamber of Commerce and Tourist Center, 4399 Main Avenue, Groves 77619; 409-962-3631, 800-876-3631.

Prairie Dog Chili Cook Off & World Championship of Pickled Quail Egg Eating, Grand Prairie
Traders Village, 2602 Mayfield Road, Grand Prairie 75052; 972-647-2331.

Grand Prairie Convention and Visitors Bureau, P.O. Box 531227, Grand Prairie 75051; 972-264-1558.

Red Steagall Cowboy Gathering & Western Swing Festival, Fort Worth

Fort Worth Convention and Visitors Bureau, 415 Throckmorton, Fort Worth 76102; 817-624-4741, 800-433-5747.

Renaissance Festival, Plantersville

Renaissance Festival, Route 2, Box 650, Plantersville 77363; 281-356-2178, 409-894-2516, 800-458-3455.

Rice Festival, Winnie

Winnie Area Chamber of Commerce, P.O. Box 147, Winnie 77665; 409-296-2231.

Sassafras Festival, San Augustine County

San Augustine County Chamber of Commerce, 611 West Columbia, San Augustine 95972; 409-275-3610.

Scarborough Faire, the Renaissance Festival, Waxahachie

Scarborough Faire, P.O. Box 538, Waxahachie 75168; 972-938-3247.

Shrimporee, Aransas Pass

Aransas Pass Chamber of Commerce, 452 West Cleveland, Aransas Pass 78336; 512-758-3713, 800-633-3028.

Spinach Festival, Crystal City

Crystal City Festival Association, P.O. Box 100, Crystal City 78839; 830-374-3161.

Strawberry Festival, Poteet

Poteet Strawberry Festival, P.O. Box 227, Poteet 78065; 210-742-8144.

Tomato Fest, Jacksonville

Jacksonville Chamber of Commerce, P.O. Box 1231, Jacksonville 75766; 903-586-2217, 800-376-2217.

Uncle Fletch's Hamburger Cook-off & American Music Festival, Henderson County

Central Business Association of Athens, P.O. Box 2773, Athens 75751.

Athens Convention and Visitors Bureau, P.O. Box 2600, Athens 75751; 903-675-5181.

Watermelon Thump, Luling

Luling Watermelon Thump Association, Box 710, Luling 76848; 830-875-3214.

Western Heritage Classic and Ranch Rodeo, Abilene

Abilene Convention and Visitors Bureau, 1101 North 1st, Abilene 79601; 915-676-2556, 800-727-7704.

Wine and Food Festival, San Angelo

San Angelo Cultural Affairs Council, P.O. Box 2477, San Angelo 76902; 915-653-6793.

San Angelo Convention and Visitors Bureau, 500 Rio Concho Drive, San Angelo 76903; 915-653-3162, 800-375-1206.

World's Largest Rattlesnake Round-up, Sweetwater

Rattlesnake Round-Up, P.O. Box 416, Sweetwater 79556; 915-235-5488.

Sweetwater Chamber of Commerce Convention and Visitors Bureau, P.O. Box 1148, Sweetwater 79556; 915-235-5488, 800-658-6757.

Wurstfest, New Braunfels

Wurstfest Association of New Braunfels, P.O. Box 310309, New Braunfels 78131-0309; 830-625-9167, 800-221-4369.

New Braunfels Convention and Visitors Bureau, P.O. Box 311417, New Braunfels 78131; 210-625-2385, 800-572-2626.

Yamboree, Gilmer

East Texas Yamboree, P.O. Box 854, Gilmer 75644; 903-843-2413.

INDEX

ABOUT THE AUTHOR

Books by Bob Carter

The Best of Central California: Main Roads & Side Trips

Soup's On! Hot Recipes from Cook Chefs (with Gail Hobbs)

Food Festivals of Northern California: Traveler's Guide & Cookbook

Food Festivals of Southern California: Traveler's Guide & Cookbook

Bob Carter is an award-winning print and electronic media author and journalist. His ongoing articles and columns appear in a variety of magazines, newspapers, and websites. He served on the faculty of Pasadena City College; California State University, Los Angeles; and the University of Oregon. A native of California and a four-year resident of Texas, he currently resides in California's central coast region.

Long devoted to traveling in a recreation vehicle, Carter has traveled more than 125,000 highway miles around the United States meeting people, visiting travel attractions, and attending large city and small town festivals and events. His books are drawn from his extensive firsthand travel experiences and adventures.